Niklaus Rudolf Schweizer

The Ut pictura poesis
Controversy in Eighteenth-Century
England and Germany

European University Papers

Europäische Hochschulschriften
Publications Universitaires Européennes

Series XVIII

Comparative literature

Reihe XVIII   Série XVIII

Vergleichende Literaturwissenschaften
Littérature comparée

Vol./Bd. 2

Niklaus Rudolf Schweizer

The Ut pictura poesis
Controversy in Eighteenth-Century
England and Germany

Herbert Lang Bern & Peter Lang Frankfurt/M.
1972

Niklaus Rudolf Schweizer

The Ut pictura poesis Controversy in Eighteenth–Century England and Germany

Herbert Lang Bern & Peter Lang Frankfurt/M.
1972

ISBN 3 261 00222 0

©

Herbert Lang & Co. Ltd., Bern (Switzerland)
Peter Lang Ltd., Frankfurt/M. (West-Germany)
1972. All rights reserved.

Printed by Lang Druck Ltd., Liebefeld/Berne (Switzerland)

"Man muss Jüngling sein, um sich zu vergegenwärtigen, welche Wirkung Lessings Laokoon auf uns ausübte, indem dieses Werk uns aus der Region eines kümmerlichen Anschauens in die freien Gefilde des Gedankens hinriss. Das so lange missverstandene ut pictura poesis war auf einmal beseitigt, der Unterschied der bildenden und Redekünste klar, die Gipfel beider erschienen nun getrennt, wie nahe ihre Basen auch zusammenstossen mochten. Der bildende Künstler sollte sich innerhalb der Grenzen des Schönen halten, wenn dem redenden, der die Bedeutung jeder Art nicht entbehren kann, auch darüber hinauszuschweifen vergönnt war."

Goethe, Dichtung und Wahrheit

TABLE OF CONTENTS

CHAPTER I

THE TRADITIONAL UT PICTURA POESIS POSITION

1. INTRODUCTION

One of the favorite topics of poets, painters, and critics in the eighteenth century was the concept of "the sister arts," or, to use Horace's famous expression ut pictura poesis. At least as much energy was spent on this subject as on "taste," the "sublime," the "beautiful," and related concepts of aesthetic interest. Ut pictura poesis suggested that all the arts are very similar, that they represent merely different facets of the same universal phenomenon. Poetry, painting, sculpture, and to some extent music were considered to be closely related and under certain conditions even interchangeable. Throughout the century there was a definite tendency in England as well as on the Continent to judge painting by the standards of literature and vice versa. Joseph Spence in his Polymetis: or, An Enquiry concerning the Agreement between the Works of the Roman Poets, and the Remains of the Antient Artists (1), for instance, maintained persistently that no subject was appropriate in poetry unless it could be represented successfully in painting or sculpture. Anne-Claude-Philippe de Tubière, Comte de Caylus, went even further to urge the "writing" of an Iliad in the form of paintings inspired by a succession of paintable scenes. (2) Indeed, the age abounded with typical ut pictura poesis statements, and the theme has been duly taken up by modern scholarship. (3)

Modern critics point out that the eighteenth century basically believed in a close relationship of poetry, painting, and music. They elaborate on the links that exist between this critical tenet and the rise of the nature poetry of James Thomson, the literary tableaux of William Collins and Thomas Gray, and the landscapes of Joseph Turner, Thomas Girtin, and John Constable. What they generally overlook, however, is that the ut pictura poesis concept was never universally held. On the contrary a reaction against it began to gain ground in the late seventeenth and the early eighteenth century which can be traced back to two Renaissance critics, Leonardo da Vinci and his countryman Benedetto Varchi. This reaction found support in a number of eighteenth-century critics, most of them English, and finally culminated in Gotthold Ephraim Lessing's Laokoon in 1766.

This thesis proposes to examine the rising opposition to ut pictura poesis and attempts to trace its development. Lessing is universally credited for having differentiated between the arts, but modern scholars have surprisingly little to say about the tradition which was behind him and which enabled him to reach his conclusions. If they refer to any possible precursors at all, they usually choose only one or two and dismiss the subject with a few brief remarks.

Only a handful of critics are somewhat more informative. William G. Howard in "Burke among the Forerunners of Lessing" (4) is such an exception. He treats the possible influences of Edmund Burke on Lessing at length and mentions even that James Harris's Three Treatises (1744) could have provided Lessing with insights that enabled him to differentiate between the arts. But Howard's attempt, though remarkable, is too limited in scope. The German Oskar Walzel in Poesie und Nichtpoesie (5) discounts Harris's influence and points out, erroneously it seems, that Lessing found all the essential elements of his aesthetic doctrine already in Shaftesbury's "A Notion of the Historical Draught or Tablature of the Judgment of Hercules" in the second edition of the Characteristics of Men, Manners, Opinions, Times. Bruno Markwardt in Geschichte der deutschen Poetik, (6) one of the standard works of modern German criticism, tends to agree with Walzel. Ralph Cohen in a chapter entitled "Things, Images and Imagination : The Reconsideration of Description" in The Art of Discrimination (7) lists a few eighteenth century critics who cautioned against the unlimited use of poetic description which was promoted by the ut pictura poesis school. Cohen, however, does not establish the obvious link that existed between such a stand against tedious description and the growing reaction to the concept of "the sister arts."

Thus, even the more thorough critics are not quite adequate in their treatment of the relationship of the arts in the eighteenth century. Jean Hagstrum's The Sister Arts; the Tradition of Literary Pictorialism and English Poetry from Dryden to Gray probably demonstrates best the need for a close investigation of the development of the opposition to ut pictura poesis. Hagstrum carries the "sister arts" concept so far that he attempts to force even Lessing into this category. He finds in the Laokoon a "concession of evident truth to the notion that poetry is a speaking picture and painting a silent poem." (8) Nothing would have been further removed from Lessing's mind than such an admission.

Obviously a new approach to the subject is called for, an approach that does not accept ut pictura poesis as an overwhelmingly acclaimed critical position, but rather sees it in the light of a controversy which steadily increased as the age unfolded. Such a new way of looking at this aesthetic problem changes also the evaluation of Lessing. He does not appear any more as the sole opponent of a timehonored critical idea; he is the clear mind that was able to combine the various elements of a rising reaction to ut pictura poesis into a firm theory that has so far withstood the test of time to an amazing extent. But before this reaction and its results can be investigated, it is necessary to sketch the traditional ut pictura poesis position toward which it was directed.

2. THE ORIGIN OF THE UT PICTURA POESIS DOCTRINE

Everyone agrees that Horace coined the famous expression, although Hagstrum shows that Plutarch in his Moralia attributed a very similar phrase to Simonides of Ceos, who allegedly had said that "painting is mute poetry, and poetry a speaking picture." (9) Cicero had also pointed out in the Tusculan Disputations that Homer really had created paintings, not poems, in spite of the fact that he was generally held to have been blind. (10) Nevertheless, ut pictura poesis is found for the first time in the Ars poetica. The passage in which it appears deserves to be quoted:

verum operi longo fas est obrepere somnum.
ut pictura poesis: erit quae si propious stes
te capiat magis, et quaedam si longius abstes,

> haec amat obscurum, volet haec sub luce videri,
> iudicis argutum quae non formidat acumen;
> haec placuit semel, haec decies repetita placebit. (11)

Horace, then, merely pointed out that in painting as well as in poetry there are good works and bad works, works which can be seen in broad daylight and always please, and others which, though protected by the shade, please only once. To derive a theory of the close relationship of poetry, the plastic arts, and even music from such a vague passage seems to be rather contrived. But as Hagstrum demonstrates convincingly, the punctuation was significantly altered in the editions of the fifteenth and part of the sixteenth century, so that the crucial line read: "ut pictura poesis erit ...", instead of "ut pictura poesis: erit quae ..." (12) This made the phrase more forceful: "a poem will be like a painting," instead of the weaker "it will be sometimes the case that ..."

At any rate, the Renaissance eagerly elaborated on Horace's thought. A number of Italian critics speculated about the close links they believed to exist between poetry and the pictorial arts. In 1436 Leon Battista Alberti (1404 - 1472) drew a parallel between painting and poetry in a study entitled Della Pittura. (13) Alberti maintained that the poets influenced the painters through their allegories and through successful descriptions. Homer's description of Zeus, for example, inspired Phidias to shape his famous gold and ivory statue of the god, which graced the temple of Olympia.

Giovanni Giorgio Trissino (1478 - 1550) in his Poetica (1529) pursued a line similar to Alberti, and so did his contemporary Bernardino Daniello (d. 1563) in La Poetica (1536). Julius Caesar Scaliger (1484 - 1558) deduced from Aristotle and Plato that all oration is based on image, idea, and imitation. This, he reasoned, is as true in rhetoric as it is in painting:

> Omnis enim oratio ειδος, εννοια, μιμησις,
> quemadmodum et pictura: id quod et ab Aristotele et a
> Platone declaratum est. (14)

Carl Heinrich von Stein maintains that this passage expresses a basic rule imposed by painting on poetry, namely, that a poet can imitate only like a painter. Thus he has to restrict himself to certain specified objects found in nature:

> Scaliger verbindet die Aristotelische μιμησις mit dem
> fernerhin unzählige Male zitierten Horazischen Worte
> ut pictura poesis. Von der Malerei auf die Poesie
> übertragen, ergibt sich dann aus dem Begriffe des
> Nachahmens eine Forderung. Man ahme so nach, wie der
> Maler nachahmt; d.h. man halte sich an bestimmte
> gegebene Gegenstände, man bilde die Natur ab. (15)

It seems that von Stein read an idea into Scaliger's work which was not necessarily there. His method of arguing, however, is noteworthy, precisely because in its freedom of interpretation it is so typical of the ut pictura poesis school. The many critics who in the course of history have based their aesthetic theories on Horace's phrase, a phrase which Hagstrum calls "one of the most frequently cited texts of ancient criticism," (16) have one common ground, namely, the idea that painting is like poetry. From this premise they deduce an astonishing variety of consequences, not infrequently involving themselves in rather obvious contradictions, a point that will be stressed in Chapter II.

In the Renaissance Giovanni Paolo Lomazzo (b. 1538) undoubtedly went farthest in demonstrating the validity of Horace's statement. While his contemporaries usually contented themselves with a few generalizations on the close relationship of the arts, Lomazzo carried ut pictura poesis to the very limits, as it were. In his Trattato dell'arte de la Pittura (1584), which was translated into English by Richard Haydocke in 1598, he filled many a page with quotations of "poetic pictures" in poets ranging from Homer to Ariosto.

The concept of "the sister arts" apparently reached England in 1586. It is interesting to know that it was not Horace's word which gave rise to the first English comment on the close connection between poet and painter, but the much clearer phrase that Simonides had allegedly coined some 500 years earlier. The reference can be found in Sir Edward Hoby's translation of the Instruction aux Princes pour garder la Foy promise: contenant un sommaire de la philosophie Chrestienne et morale ... en plusieurs discours politiques sur la verité & le mensonge, written by Matthieu Coignet, sieur de la Thuillerie (1514 - 1586) in 1584:

> For as Simonides saide: Painting is a dumme Poesie,
> and a Poesie is a speaking painting: & the actions
> which the Painters set out with visible colours and
> figures the Poets recken with wordes, as though they
> had in deede been perfourmed. (17)

In the seventeenth century a number of English poets and critics referred to ut pictura poesis. Ben Johnson, George Puttenham, Edmund Spenser, and George Chapman all devoted a paragraph or two to the problem. But the first extended treatise did not appear until 1695, when John Dryden published his translation of Charles Alphonse Du Fresnoy's Latin poem De arte graphica. Du Fresnoy had written the poem in Rome sometime between 1633 and 1653. It had been translated into French by Roger de Piles in 1668. Du Fresnoy intended to do for painting what Horace had done for poetry; namely, to establish an authoritative critical theory. Dryden found the poem interesting enough to deserve not only a translation, but also an introduction in the form of a lengthy essay which he prefixed to the translation. "A Parallel between Painting and Poetry" represented a careful study of the similarities of the two arts. (18) As such it became the very basis for the innumerable discussions of ut pictura poesis that increasingly flowed from the press as the eighteenth century progressed. Ironically enough, it also contained a passage which Lessing recognized as a starting point for his theory which refutes the validity of "the sister arts" concept.

Since Du Fresnoy's poem was meant as an apologia for painting, an art which had generally been considered inferior to poetry and which indeed continued to be seen in this light well into the eighteenth century, it is not surprising that Dryden in his preface applied the rules of painting to poetry, and not vice versa, as was usually the case. At this point a short discussion on the widespread customs of the Enlightenment to rank the arts according to merit seems to be appropriate.

3. RANKING THE ARTS

As every student of the eighteenth century knows, the age had a fondness for order and regularity. A hierarchical system inherited from the middle ages controlled the organization of the state, the church, the military services, and indeed of society in general. This principle was so firmly entrenched in the minds of the English that in an upper class household, to give an amusing example, there prevailed a very definite hierarchy "below stairs." The butler took the place of the lord of the house, the housekeeper of the lady, while the first gentleman's gentleman occupied a considerably higher level on the scale of status, than did the personal servant of the second oldest son. It does not surprise, then, that a similar system was applied to the arts.

In the realm of the arts the tendency to establish a hierarchy can be already seen in the Italian Renaissance. Leonardo da Vinci and his contemporaries had engaged in so-called "paragoni," or contests of critical arguments. Such contests were held not only between poets and painters, but also between sculptors and poets, and even between the representatives of the arts of Florence and those of Venice. Leonardo's Trattato della Pittura, for example, was written to vindicate the position of the painter, who since antiquity had been held inferior to the poet.

Du Fresnoy espoused the cause of Leonardo, and so did Jonathan Richardson (1665 - 1745), well known in his time as the portraitist of Milton, Newton, Pope, and Prior, in his three essays (1715) entitled "The Theory of Painting"; "Essay on the Art of Criticism, so far as it relates to Painting"; "The Science of a Connoisseur". The famous French Abbé Dubos in the Réflexions critiques sur la poësie et sur la peinture (1719) followed suit. To be precise, Dubos did not try to maintain the supremacy of painting over poetry, but was content to point out that painting was not inferior but rather on the same level with its famous sister. Richardson, however, made it quite clear that he preferred painting to poetry. In "The Science of a Connoisseur" he entertains the reader with the following hierarchy governing the arts:

> Thus, history begins, poetry raises higher, not
> only by embellishing the story, but by additions
> purely poetical: Sculpture goes yet farther,
> and painting compleats and perfects, and that only
> can; and here ends; this is the utmost limit of
> human power in the communication of ideas. (19)

And he adds that "the business of painting is to do almost all that discourse and books can, in many instances, much more, as well as more speedily and more delightfully; ..." (pp. 264 - 265). But the great majority of Richardson's contemporaries would have agreed with him only in his assertion that the business of a painting was to tell a story, for this was the age of historical painting and portraits. Painting as such, however, was generally regarded as a younger and less accomplished sister of poetry. The average critic held that painting could do everything that poetry did, but in a limited if not inferior way.

As a result of this prevailing view, the painter occupied a considerably lower station than the poet during the first half of the eighteenth century. William Hogarth and especially Sir Joshua Reynolds gradually improved the painter's lot, so that he reached an equal footing with the poet towards the end of the century. But in the meantime the painter had to be content with a lower rung on the social ladder.

The French drew an even more clear-cut line between painters and poets. Remy G. Saisselin demonstrates this in an amusing anecdote. Referring to a sudden improvement in the social position of the French artist in the middle of the eighteenth century he writes:

> The unprecedented feat of receiving painters,
> sculptors, and engravers socially, on a footing
> equal to that already gained by men of letters,
> was due to Madame Geoffrin and the Comte Caylus.
> This lady was pleased to receive artists and the
> amateur count on Mondays, for dinner, to be
> followed by conversation in the afternoon. But note
> that men of letters were received on another day,
> Wednesday. (20)

Saisselin goes on to remark that the rivalry between "the pen and the brush" deepened again in the seventh decade of the century with the antagonistic positions taken up by Denis Diderot and the sculptor Etienne-Maurice Falconet.

It seems that for the better part of the century there was a widespread tendency on the part of men of letters to look at painters and sculptors with a certain amount of contempt as less educated and poorly read people, as mere "artisans" instead of "artists." As a result some of the exponents of the plastic arts attempted to cultivate the poetical muse on the side, in order to gain in their social standing. Falconet and Maurice Quentin de la Tour tried to do some social climbing through this method. The undisputed master of both painting and writing was Reynolds, of course. He advised painters to solicit the company of poets, writers, and critics, in order to improve their learning and to find ideas for future pictures. Comte Caylus argued in the same vein and emphasized the great pleasure that an artist could find in reading a good author:

> Quel plaisir pour un peintre, en se délassant de
> ses occupations ordinaires, d'aller pour ainsi
> dire à la découverte dans un bon auteur! Oui,

Messieurs, vous devez goûter un attrait bien plus
vif que tous les hommes à lire ces historiens, ces
poètes, où tout est, pour l'ordinaire, en action. (21)

The painter's equality as a creative artist was brought about, at last, and
the competition between poetry and painting faded away. Saisselin puts it as follows:

> By the end of the [eighteenth] century literature
> no longer held undisputed sway over the imagination
> of men and no longer enjoyed the privileged position
> it formerly held vis-à-vis the visual arts. Painting,
> and that elusive quality poetry, associated with
> painting, had become serious rivals to letters, but
> the end of this story was written only in the
> nineteenth century. (22)

At the same time ended the disputes concerning the place of music, as
well as of various other disciplines that the age summed up under the term "art,"
for that word was by no means limited to poetry, painting, sculpture, architecture, and music. James Harris's Three Treatises (1744) demonstrates the
extensive interpretation the age was pleased to apply to this word. James Harris,
better known as "Hermes Harris", added to the five conventional arts listed
above such activities as agriculture, gardening, navigation (piloting), weapon
making, and the taming of animals, as well as the hunting of those beasts that
do not submit to being tamed. (23)

4. THE DEVELOPMENT OF UT PICTURA POESIS AFTER DRYDEN

As mentioned above, Dryden's preface to his translation of De arte graphica directed the attention of many English writers to the concept of "the sister
arts." But Dryden's essay was not the only cause of the sudden increase in the
popularity this subject met with around the turn of the century. The roots, indeed, go deeper, and can be found in the source for all of the aesthetic pursuits
that interested the Enlightenment, namely, the empirical philosophy of Thomas
Hobbes, John Locke, and, later, David Hume. Empiricism challenged the efficacy of reason and exalted the importance of sense perception. It resulted in a
growing interest in psychology, in a desire to illuminate the functions of the
mind. The attention was gradually shifted from the investigation of the nature of
objects to the ways the human mind perceives them and reacts to them, or to
speak with Ronald S. Crane, the academic limelight was turned from "art" to
the "audience." (24) Samuel H. Monk has effectively described this crucial shift
in critical interest:

Under a great variety of titles, a great variety

of men at one time or other [in the eighteenth
century] composed an essay or a book or a poem on
taste or beauty or sublimity or the pleasures of
the imagination or the art of poetry, of painting,
or of music. Not everyone who wrote had something
to say, but on the part of both philosopher and
connoisseur (and most fine gentlemen had a "taste")
considerable interest was manifested in the questions
of why objects are beautiful and how these objects
affect one. On the part of the philosophers this
was probably due to the emphasis which empiricism
had placed on sensation, with the resultant interest
in psychology of a rudimentary sort; as for the
connoisseur, he was doubtless merely following a
fashion in philosophy in an age when cultivated
leisure permitted every gentleman to take pen in
hand. (25)

The ut pictura poesis theory was just as much affected by the new philosophy as were the concepts of "beauty," "sublimity," the "ridiculous," etc., as
well as the all-encompassing concept of "taste." The exact nature of this influence, of course, is complex and has not yet been studied in all its ramifications.
Dryden's essay, then, fortified by the empirical philosophy with its emphasis on sense perception, resulted in a great number of paragraphs and essays
on "the sister arts." Of these numerous, often second-rate productions we will
select only one for a more detailed discussion, an essay attributed to Sir Richard
Blackmore (1654 - 1729). The essay deserves attention simply because it is so
typical for the unreserved adherence to ut pictura poesis on the part of many,
though by no means all, eighteenth century critics and connoisseurs. It originally
appeared in two consecutive numbers of the Lay Monastery on January 25 and 27,
1713, under the title of "Parallel between poetry and painting."
To make certain that no one would miss the point, Sir Richard selected
as a motto for his essay ut pictura poesis, as well as a quotation from George
Colman, playwright and translator of Horace: "Poems and Pictures are adjudged
alike." He begins with the familiar observation that of the three "sister arts,"
painting and poetry have the closest similarity:

Though the melody of the voice, and that of
musical instruments, bear a great resemblance to
the charms of Poetry, as they are expressed in
harmonious numbers, and a pleasing cadence of
words; yet the affinity between Poetry and
Painting must be allowed to be much greater. (26)

Blackmore concedes that poetry is directed to hearing, painting to sight.
But he contrives to dispel any potential doubts in the close relationship between
the two arts which may arise from this difference by the skillful application of

poetic terms to painting and pictorial ones to poetry:

> The painter is a poet to the eye, and a poet a
> painter to the ear. One gives us pleasure by
> silent eloquence, the other by vocal imagery. One
> shews the art of drawing and colouring by the pen,
> the other with equal elegance expresses a poetical
> spirit by the pencil. When a poet has formed an
> admirable description of a palace, a river, or a
> grove, the reader in transport cries, what a fine
> painting is this! (p. 33)

The last sentence of this paragraph is quite significant, since it demonstrates the
great weight the ut pictura poesis school put on poetic description. It will be shown
in Chapter II that description was one of the cornerstones of the school, and that
the growing opposition to the ut pictura poesis theory did begin with a stand against
tediously long descriptions. Lessing himself later devotes a great deal of attention to the problems centering around poetic description.

    Sir Richard proceeds to find in poetry analogies to the various categories
of painting. "Grotesque painting" corresponds to humorous ballads, farces and
burlesque verse, landscape painting to pastoral poetry, portrait painting to the
kind of descriptive poetry that celebrates the face and charms of Lesbia, as
drawn by Horace, or Laura, as represented by Petrarch (pp. 33 - 34).

    As might be expected, Blackmore finds the closest resemblance between
history painting and the epic, as well as tragedy, those genres of painting and
literature, which the age generally praised as the most valuable. In this connection Raphael is mentioned as a great "poet, " and Virgil as an equally great "painter":

> What poetical design and description, what an epic
> imagination does Raphael shew in his celebrated
> piece of Constantine and Maxentius! and what
> masterly and admirable painting does Virgil express,
> when he describes the battle of the Latins and the
> Trojans! (p. 35)

Blackmore adds another assertion typical of ut pictura poesis, namely,
that painters often obtain their ideas from poets, and poets from painters. Blackmore deduces:

> The masters of the pencil often take their ideas,
> and borrow the passions they would exhibit, from
> the writings of the poet; while the painter is
> himself but the copyist, and the poet the original.
> 'Tis observed of Raphael, the most famous in his
> art, that he formed the Jupiter in his Psyche, by
> the admirable description of that deity in Virgil,

when Venus addressed her petition to him. Nor is
the poet, in his turn, less obliged to the great
pieces of the painter, who often sits to the poet,
while he forms his ideas; and, inspired by the lively
and passionate figures expressed in colours, translates the painter, and turns the pictures into
verse.' (p. 38)

Blackmore also points out that the poet, as well as the painter, uses alle-
gory to make a greater impression on the reader or the spectator (pp. 38 - 39).
They should both deal with only one sustained action, and they should both compose a work of didactic value (p. 40). However, both painting and poetry have
a far greater aesthetic effect than a moral one, so that the former often renders
the latter ineffectual (p. 41).

Sir Richard really sees but one essential difference between poetry and
painting, and that is that time increases the value of a great picture, whereas
this is not always the case with poetry, "since time often obscures rather than
beautifies the diction of the poet." (p. 42) Nevertheless, this does not necessarily prevent posterity from paying a higher tribute to a poet than did his contemporaries. Blackmore mentions Milton who was neglected in his own days,
but "whose poem ... is justly acknowledged to be the most admirable produc-
tion of British genius, ..." (p. 42).

Finally, the parallel between poetry and painting holds also in the region
of bathos, a region which Blackmore seems to define in terms of a conspicuous
lack of morals. In those realms the painters of lascivious Jupiters and the like
meet with immoral writers in common debauchery (pp. 43 - 44).

Blackmore's essay is a case in point for the very core of the ut pictura
poesis school. Although he is inclined to favor painting at the expense of poetry,
whereas poetry was normally regarded as the more mature sister, he is remarkably consistent in his main argument, much more so than certain other writers
on the same subject. Theoreticians such as Joseph Trapp (1679 - 1747) and
Hildebrand Jacob (1693 - 1739), who on the surface seem to subscribe to "the
sister arts" doctrine, turn out to be quite contradictory when examined more
carefully. Notwithstanding its title, Jacob's little book Of the Sister Arts (1734)
really belongs to the reaction to ut pictura poesis and will, therefore, deserve
careful attention.

5. POETIC DESCRIPTION

The most important aspect of the traditional ut pictura poesis view was
the emphasis placed on poetic description. Since poetry and painting were held
to be really the same, it is easy to see why poetic description occupied a favorite
place in this critical system. Painting imitated nature directly through the use of
colors and figures; it "described" nature. Poetry, therefore, was to do the same.
It was supposed to "describe" likewise, not with colors, but with words, through

the enumeration of particulars. The author of an essay in the <u>Lay Monastery</u>, No. 39, Feb. 12, 1713, who is identified by Ralph Cohen as John Hughes (1677 - 1720) (27), states the case for description quite clearly: "There are no parts in a poem which strike the generality of readers with so much pleasure as descriptions; ...". (28) He then continues:

> The reason why descriptions make livelier impressions
> on common readers than any other parts of a poem, is
> because they are formed of ideas drawn from the
> senses, which is sometimes too called imaging, and
> are thus in a manner, like pictures, made objects of
> the sight: whereas, moral thoughts and discourses,
> consisting of ideas abstracted from sense, operate
> slower and with less vivacity. Every one immediately
> perceives the resemblance of nature in the description
> of a tempest, a palace, or a garden; but the beauty of
> proper sentiments in the speeches of a prince, a
> general, or a counsellor, is more remote, and dis-
> cerned by a kind of second thought or reflection.
> (pp. 45 - 46)

Lessing in his <u>Laokoon</u> was to prove that precisely the sentiments and not the tedious enumeration of details made up the beauty of a poem. But Hughes's argument is very typical and can be found in dozens of critics.

Anthony Blackwell (1674 - 1730), for example, wrote in 1718 that "lively description" is "a figure of speech" that communicates "such a strong and beautiful Representation of a thing, as gives the Reader a distinct View and satisfactory Notion of it." (29) Joseph Trapp (1679 - 1747), a theoretician not necessarily known for his consistency, emphasizes in the following passage the value of poetic description and establishes an interesting link between description and metaphor:

> I would here, however, particularly observe, that
> Poetry consists much more in Description, than is
> generally imagined. For, besides those longer and
> set Descriptions of Things, Places, and Persons, there
> are numberless others, unobserved by common Readers,
> contained in one Verse, sometimes in one Word, to
> which the whole Beauty of the Thought is owing;
> and which wonderfully affect us, for no other Reason
> but because they are Descriptions, that is, impress
> a lively Image of somewhat upon the Mind. To this
> it is, that metaphorical Expressions, when selected
> with Judgment, owe their Beauty, and their Elegance;
> every Metaphor being a short Description. (30)

Many more examples could be given, but it suffices to add only one, taken from <u>Humphry Clinker</u>. Smollett has Matthew Bramble send a copy of the <u>Ode to Leven</u>

<u>Water</u>, a descriptive poem, full of pastoral clichés, to his correspondent, Dr. Lewis. In the accompanying letter Mr. Bramble shows his predilection for descriptive poetry:

> Enclosed I send you the copy of a little ode to
> this river, by Dr. Smollett [sic], who was born on
> the banks of it, within two miles of the place where
> I am now writing. It is at least picturesque and
> accurately descriptive, if it has no other merit.
> There is an idea of truth, in an agreeable landscape
> taken from nature, which pleases me more than the
> gayest fiction which the most luxuriant fancy can
> display. (31)

The cause of poetic description derived great support from two theoreticians who had an undisputed influence on the eighteenth century, John Locke and Joseph Addison. Locke in a chapter entitled "Of Study," in his <u>Thoughts on Education</u> (1693) had argued the necessity of clearing up the prevailing linguistic confusion. He had warned against an undue concern in mere "words," as opposed to the "things" they actually stand for. He had gone as far as to propose a new way of thinking, based entirely on the objects themselves without taking recourse to words:

> ... for words are, in their own nature, so doubtful
> and obscure, their signification for the most part,
> so uncertain and undetermined which men even designedly
> have in their use of them increased, that if in our
> meditation our thoughts busy themselves with words,
> and stick at the names of things, it is odds but
> they are misled and confounded. (32)

Locke was thus in favor of a language as simple and direct as possible, a language that would correspond in the number of words to the objects the speaker or writer had in mind. Now, it is quite evident that the description of a mountain or river lends itself more easily to Locke's linguistic ideas, than does an account of the wrath of Achilles or the jealousy of Medea.

Locke, of course, was not alone in demanding a reform of language. Already Thomas Hobbes, and to some extent Sir Francis Bacon had done so, and the Royal Society had been preoccupied with it to such an extent that Jonathan Swift's ridicule was provoked in the well-known account of the "school of languages" in the third book of <u>Gulliver's Travels</u>.

The development of poetic description into a major concern derived strength from another source, Addison's essays on "The Pleasures of the Imagination" in <u>The Spectator</u>, Nos. 411 - 421. Addison, under the influence of Hobbesian and Lockian empiricism, emphasized the role of the senses, especially of sight, in starting the imagination working.

> It is this Sense [sight] which furnishes the
> Imagination with its Ideas; so that by the
> Pleasures of the Imagination or Fancy (which I
> shall use promiscuously) I here mean such as arise
> from visible Objects, either when we have them
> actually in our View, or when we call up their Ideas
> into our Minds by Paintings, Statues, Descriptions
> [my italics] , or any the like Occasion. (33)

It is easy to see the connection between imagination and poetic description in Addison's scheme. If the pleasures of the imagination are based on the sense of sight, then description will contribute a major share to these pleasures. It is hardly surprising, then, that Addison refers to the efficacy of description several times. Comparing the pleasures of reason to the enjoyments derived from the imagination he writes:

> A beautiful Prospect delights the Soul, as much as
> a Demonstration; and a Description in Homer has
> charmed more Readers than a Chapter in Aristotle.
> (p. 538)

Or he states:

> A Man of a Polite Imagination, is let into a great
> many Pleasures, that the Vulgar are not capable of
> receiving. He can converse with a Picture, and find
> an agreeable Companion in a Statue. He meets with a
> secret Refreshment in a Description, and often feels
> a greater Satisfaction in the Prospect of Fields and
> Meadows, than another does in the Possession. (Ibid.)

And in another passage he juxtaposes painting and poetry in the light of description, thus demonstrating what has been established above, namely that description in all likelihood was the most important aspect of the ut pictura poesis theory:

> We might here add, that the Pleasures of the Fancy (34)
> are more conducive to Health, than those of the
> Understanding, which are worked out by Dint of
> Thinking, and attended with too violent a Labour
> of the Brain. Delightful Scenes, whether in Nature,
> Painting, or Poetry, have a kindly Influence on
> the Body, as well as the Mind, and not only serve
> to clear and brighten the Imagination, but are able
> to disperse Grief and Melancholly, and to set the
> Animal Spirit in pleasing and agreeable Motions.
> (p. 539)

Thus, poetical description derived its justification from a philosophical and an aesthetic source, a powerful combination indeed. It is no coincidence that James Thomson introduced a new poetic genre with his <u>Winter</u> in 1726. The foundations for "nature poetry" had been well prepared both by poetic forerunners such as Milton, Denham, Dyer, and Pope, as well as by the <u>ut pictura poesis</u> school.

By now it has become clear that the concept of "the sister arts" was not a purely academic matter, but had implications which far exceeded the limited interests of pedantic theoreticians. It encouraged the poets not only to include lengthy descriptions in their works, but to found a new kind of poetry altogether. Similarly, the concept influenced painting. In the first half of the century the allegorical picture, the picture that tells a story, became the fashion, a trend that was carried to its logical extreme by Hogarth's pictorial "novels." Towards the end of the century the attention in England shifted to landscape painting after Italian, French, and Dutch artists had led the way. (35)

6. THE ATTITUDE OF THE GERMAN AESTHETICIANS BEFORE LESSING

A close examination of the leading German aestheticians before Lessing and his mentor Moses Mendelssohn reveals that they all adhered to <u>ut pictura poesis</u>, although a certain uneasiness concerning the degree of similarity of the "sisters" is quite noticeable. Alexander Gottlieb Baumgarten (1714 - 1762), the founder of "aesthetics" as a branch of learning, (36) his student Georg Friedrich Meier (1718 - 1777), as well as Johann Jacob Bodmer (1698 - 1783) and his friend and collaborator Johann Jacob Breitinger (1701 - 1776) believed that the arts were closely related. Here and there, however, they showed signs of an awareness that the <u>ut pictura poesis</u> theory had certain limitations.

Thus Baumgarten, whose dissertation entitled <u>Meditationes philosophicae de nonnullis ad poema pertinentibus</u> (1734), written in the stilted, stiffly logical Latin used by eighteenth century German scholars, has been recently translated into English (37), carefully establishes the validity of Horace's famous statement by synthesizing a number of his earlier deductions:

> & 39. It is the function of a picture to represent
> a composite, and that is poetic, & 24; the repre-
> sentation of a picture is very similar to the sense
> idea to be depicted, and this is poetic, & 38.
> Therefore, a poem and a picture are similar, & 30.
> Ut pictura poesis. (38)

But in the following paragraph Baumgarten is quick to introduce an observation which renders the above chain of reasoning rather questionable:

> & 40. Since a picture represents an image only on a
> surface, it is not for the picture to represent every

aspect, or any motion at all; yet it is poetic to do
so, because when these things are also represented,
then more things are represented in the object than
when they are not, and hence the representing is
extensively clearer, & 16. Therefore, in poetic images
more things tend toward unity than in pictures. Hence
a poem is more perfect than a picture. (p. 52)

It becomes evident that a painting cannot depict motion, whereas a poem can, a
point that later plays a central role in Lessing's distinction of the arts. Motion
and what could be called the "universal" character of language lift poetry above
painting, according to Baumgarten. It seems that plenitude is the goal of art, a
concept which in all likelihood he derived from Gottfried Wilhelm Leibniz (1646 -
1716) and his popularizer, Christian Wolff (1679 - 1754). In & 54 Baumgarten
elaborates on this point:

& 54. By descriptions we mean enumerations of whatever parts there are in that which is represented.
Therefore, if that which is confusedly represented
is described, more parts are represented in it than
if it is not described. But if it is what we shall
call confusedly described, that is, if the confused
representations of the parts are fully supplied in the
describing, then it becomes extensively clearer. And
this is true also: the more the parts that are confusedly represented, the clearer the description is,
& 16. Therefore, confused descriptions and those
most of all in which many parts are represented are
in the highest degree poetic. (p. 56)

Admittedly, Baumgarten's logic is not easy to follow, and the many cross-refer-
ences hardly facilitate the reader's task; nevertheless, we can find in this passage
with its emphasis on obscurity a link to Edmund Burke's conception of the sublime,
and the role that language plays in communicating it. (39)
    We turn with a certain sense of relief to the clear prose of Breitinger, who
in his Critische Dichtkunst, (1740), investigated at length the nature of "poetic
painting." The full title of the work seems to suggest Breitinger's position regarding ut pictura poesis: Johann Jacob Breitingers Critische Dichtkunst Worinnen die
Poetische Mahlerey in Absicht auf die Erfindung Im Grunde untersuchet und mit
Beyspielen aus den berühmtesten Alten und Neuern erläutert wird. We thus expect
an unreserved ut pictura poesis position, but Breitinger does not live up to our
expectations. He shows himself less dogmatic than his title seems to suggest.
    To be sure, he begins by quoting Horace's famous phrase using the wrong
punctuation: Ut pictura poesis erit: Die beyden Künste, des Mahlers und des Poe-
ten sind einander sehr nahe verwandt, und gleichsam verschwistert." (40) He then
proceeds by arguing that both the painter and the poet imitate nature:

Beyde, der Mahler und der Poet, haben einerley Vorhaben,
nemlich dem Menschen abwesende Dinge als gegenwärtig
vorzustellen, und ihm dieselben gleichsam zu fühlen
und zu empfinden zu geben. Beyde arbeiten über einerley
Materie, die Wercke der Natur und der Kunst sind ihre
Urbilder, die sie durch eine geschickte Nachahmung auf
eine fühlbare Weise auszudrücken suchen. Beyde stimmen
in dem Endzwecke überein, sie wollen uns durch die
Aehnlichkeit ergetzen. Endlich haben beyde eine
Lehrmeisterin, die Natur, bey der sie in die Schule
gehen. Also bleibt übrig, dass sie alleine in der
Ausführung ihres Vorhabens unterschiden sind, da der
Mahler mit dem Pinsel und den Farben, der Poet mit den
Worten und der Feder mahlet. Aber dieser einzige
Unterschied gebiehrt ferner andere, von welchen jegliche
von diesen Künsten ihren besonderen Vortheil bekömmt.
(pp. 14 - 15)

The last two sentences are significant. Breitinger reasons that there is really
only one difference between the two arts, namely the difference of medium. The
painter paints with colors and uses the brush, the poet "paints" with words and
uses the pen. This one difference, however, gives birth to others, as it were,
so that each of the arts attains certain advantages.

Painting turns out to have a more immediate and more powerful effect
than poetry. This is due to the fact that the painter imitates objects directly as
they appear in nature. Furthermore, painting appeals to "that sense which has
the greatest power on the soul" (p. 15). Undoubtedly Breitinger refers here to
Addison's essays on "The Pleasures of the Imagination" and his emphasis of the
sense of sight as the most noble of the five.

Poetry, on the other hand, does not appeal to only one or two senses, but
to all, and it can present any action conceivable without any limitations whatever,
whereas painting cannot depict movement; it can only suggest it:

Der Poet mahlet nicht für das Auge allein, sondern
auch für die übrigen Sinnen, und er kan auch das
unsichtbare sichtbar machen, er giebt dem Menschen
nicht nur die vollkommenste Bildung, sondern auch die
Rede; die Thiere bekommen von ihm die unterschiedlich-
sten Handlungen, derer sie fähig sind, den Vögeln
schencket er die süsse Melodie des Gesanges; in seinen
Gemählden ist alles voll Leben und wahrer Bewegung;
seine Personen und Sachen ändern ihren Stand und ihre
Stellung in einem Augenblicke, so bald es ihm beliebet,
und er giebt sie uns ganz und von allen Seiten zu sehen.
(p. 19)

Breitinger's ideas on the difference between poetry and painting are reminiscent of the attempts of various precursors of Lessing to find a technical basis that would account for a separation of the arts. They selected as this basis an ars characteristica, or "theory of signs." This ars characteristica will be discussed later at length. For now it suffices to mention that Breitinger touches upon such a theory of signs, when he lists another major advantage of poetry, namely that it consists of words, which are "artificial signs of concepts and images," and which, therefore, affect the mind directly, and not by way of the senses:

> Endlich erhält die Poesie einen besondern Vortheil
> daher, dass sie sich in der absonderlichen Art ihrer
> Nachahmung, an statt der Farben der blossen Worte
> bedienet; denn da dieses willkührliche Zeichen der
> Begriffe und Bilder sind, die sich alleine dem Verstande
> vernehmlich machen, kan sie dadurch ihre Bilder unmittel-
> bar in das Gehirn anderer Menschen schildern, und so
> feine Gemählde verfertigen, die für die Sinne zu zart
> und unbegreiflich sind. (pp. 19 - 20)

Thus Breitinger mentions only incidentally what in a much more sophisticated form was to become the very core of Lessing's distinction of the arts.

Breitinger's friend Bodmer argues very much in the same vein in Johann Jacob Bodmers Critische Betrachtungen über die Poetischen Gemählde der Dichter, which was published just a year after Breitinger's work. Bodmer adds to Breitinger by attempting to define the relationship of sculpture to painting and poetry. Like Breitinger he adheres to the ut pictura poesis doctrine, feels a little uneasy about it, and discovers differences between the arts; but again like his colleague he does not really develop his findings. Ultimately the two critics from Zurich must be ranked among the ut pictura poesis school, though with reservations, a fact which is symbolized by their insistence on using the verb "to paint" ("mahlen") to characterize the activities of the poet.

We have seen, then, that by no means all critics who professed to adhere to ut pictura poesis did so without qualification. On the contrary, on the Continent and in England some of them were aware of certain differences of the arts, an awareness which was to lead in due time to a complete separation of "the sisters."

CHAPTER II

THE TREND TOWARD A SEPARATION OF THE ARTS

1. THE BEGINNINGS IN THE RENAISSANCE

In the first half of the century a reaction to the <u>ut</u> <u>pictura</u> <u>poesis</u> theory developed, hesitatingly at first but gaining more and more momentum as the age went on. This new trend toward a clear differentiation of the arts found its logical conclusion in Lessing's <u>Laokoon</u> (1766), a work that no modern aesthetician can afford to overlook. The roots of the opposition to the concept of "the sister arts" can already be found in the Italian Renaissance. Two influential theoreticians, Leonardo da Vinci and Benedetto Varchi, held surprisingly advanced views on the relationship of the arts and foreshadowed clearly what was to come in the distant future.

Leonardo actually wrote the earliest extended "parallel" between painting and poetry, in the first of the three parts of his <u>Trattato</u> <u>della</u> <u>Pittura</u>. The earliest publication of the master's haphazardly written notebook on painting appeared in Paris in 1651, but contained only parts two and three, which are very technical and in this context quite irrelevant. A translation into English under the title of <u>A</u> <u>Treatise</u> <u>of</u> <u>Painting</u> was published in 1721, but it was based on the 1651 edition and did not contain the significant first part. Leonardo's thoughts on the relationship of painting and poetry became known not before 1882, when Heinrich Ludwig published all three parts of the <u>Trattato</u> with a translation into German and a commentary. (1)

In the <u>Trattato</u> Leonardo appears as both a predecessor to and a counterpart of Lessing. He separates painting and poetry rather strictly, but he inclines naturally toward painting and has little esteem for poetry. It is significant that the poetry he likes least happens to be descriptive. Indeed, he skillfully uses the difficulties a poet faces, when he attempts description, to prove that poetry is far inferior to painting. Leonardo's thoughts are jotted down in that state of utter disorganization allowed only the genius, so that one gladly turns to William G. Howard's excellent paraphrase of the relevant ideas, a paraphrase which resulted from a meticulous sifting of Leonardo's rambling inspirations:

> The poet tediously enumerates the parts of a body, or
> recounts the successive stages of an action; the
> painter's representation of bodies and actions con-
> centrates all their elements into a single moment.
> If, therefore, the effect of a poem be likened to
> that of a melody sung by a single voice, the effect of
> a picture is the wonderful harmony of simultaneous
> cooperation. (2)

Here is, in embryonic form, Lessing's theory, with this exception, that Leonardo exalts the importance of painting at the expense of poetry, whereas Lessing does the opposite. True to his belief Leonardo treats the Horatian idea that painting is a kind of poetry and poetry a sort of painting in an amusingly ironic tone:

> If you call painting dumb poetry, the painter may say

that poetry is blind painting. Who are more afflicted,
the blind or the dumb? Poetry may indeed be called a
science for the blind, and painting a science for
the dumb. But even then, painting occupies the
higher rank, since it appeals to the higher sense. (3)

Painting, then, is a more valuable art than poetry because it involves the sense
of sight rather than the inferior sense of hearing. Leonardo leaves little doubt
that this is precisely the reason for the painter's claim to the highest place among
creative men:

> The eye is the highest and the most reliable of the
> organs of sense; it is the window of the soul,
> through which alone can come to man an accurate con-
> ception of creation and his place therein. The
> painter presents to the eye images exactly similar in
> appearance to natural objects; painting is the sole
> art that imitates all visible things; it is univers-
> ally and immediately intelligible without an inter-
> preter, and arouses the passions of men and animals
> as if its images were realities. (4)

Leonardo's most significant contribution to the clarification of the position
of the arts was undoubtedly his low view of descriptive poetry. As has been pointed
out in Chapter I, Addison emphasized the importance of sight in art in consequence
of Locke's empirical philosophy. This led him to stress the value of description in
poetry and it provided the ut pictura poesis school with an aesthetic basis. Two
centuries before Addison, however, Leonardo had drawn a completely different
conclusion from the same premise. Since sight is the most exalted sense, painting
is the highest form of art. The attempt to create a poetry that appeals to the sense
of sight, rather than hearing, is doomed to fail because the poet has to enumerate
laboriously what the painter represents in one single instant. Thus, poetic description cannot avoid being tedious. Lessing could not have agreed more.

Benedetto Varchi was not a universal genius of Leonardo's stature, but
nevertheless demonstrated in his Lezzioni ... sopra diverse materie, poetiche e
filosofiche a vast knowledge and great critical acumen. It is regrettable that this
valuable work was never translated into English, French, or German. Varchi devoted an interesting section in the Lezzioni to the position of the arts: "In che siano
simili et in che differenti i poeti et i pittori." (5)

Varchi begins with the old Aristotelian concept that the arts imitate nature.
He then proceeds in an ut pictura poesis vein, pointing out that great poets such
as Dante, Petrarch, and Horace employed a good many painterly terms. Suddenly,
however, he changes the direction of his argument to point out that poetry and
painting do differ, inasmuch as one imitates with words, the other with colors.
His most important statement, though, is that poetry is more concerned with expressing passions, whereas painting depicts bodies. This last point represents
the very core of Lessing's theory. Varchi has a central passage into which with

great deliberation he condensed his essential thoughts:

> ..., e così hauemo ueduto, perchè la poesia si chiama
> arte, e che è simili all pittura, perchè amendue
> imitano la natura. Ma è da notare: che il poeta
> l'imita colle parole, et i pittori co i colori,
> e quello, che è più, i poeti imitano il di dentro
> principalmente, cioè e concetti, e le passioni dell'
> animo, se bene molte uolte discriuono ancora, e quasi
> dipingono colle parole i corpi, e tutte le fattezze
> di tutte le cose così animate, come inanimate; et
> i pittori imitano principalmente il difuori, cioè
> i corpi, e le fattezze di tutte le cose. (6)

> ["..., and so we have seen, why poetry is called an
> art, and that it is similar to painting, because both
> imitate nature. But it should be noted that the poet
> imitates with words and the painters with colors, and
> furthermore that the poets imitate principally the inner
> aspects, which are the concepts and passions of the
> spirit, although many times they also describe and
> almost paint bodies with words, and all the facets of
> all things animate and inanimate; and the painters
> imitate principally the outer aspects, which are the
> bodies, and the aspects of all things."]

Thus both Leonardo and Varchi asserted that the arts had to be differentiated and that ut pictura poesis was an oversimplified idea which could not be accepted without considerable modifications. That they did not pursue their insights to the point of writing studies equal in importance to the Laokoon may be easily excused when it is considered that they worked in an environment that unreservedly accepted the theory of "the sister arts." Nevertheless, the two had worked out the basic tenets of Lessing and his eighteenth century precursors. Leonardo contributed the important idea of the punctum temporis, the concept that the painter represents the object of his picture in a single moment, with the implication that the poet works within a time-succession. Varchi added that poetry is suited to treat the passions, whereas painting depicts bodies.

This promising aesthetic development, however, was completely ignored by Leonardo's and Varchi's contemporaries. The thread was lost for a full century, and when René Rapin and René Le Bossu picked it up again, they did so in a purely coincidental way by mildly warning against unnecessarily long descriptions in pastoral and epic poetry.

2. INCREASING WARNINGS AGAINST POETIC DESCRIPTION

As we have seen in Chapter I, a number of eighteenth century scholars had praised description, in the sense of the minute enumeration of particulars, as most poetical. But not everyone shared this enthusiastic belief in description. A growing number of theoreticians and poets began to point out that the unlimited use of description could result in dullness. Rapin opposed excessive description when he advocated "sparing," or brevity, and lauded Virgil for describing the beechen pot of Meliboeus tersely, whereas Theocritus is intolerably longwinded: "Theocritus made a long immoderate description of his Cup." (7) Le Bossu was also of the opinion that abundant description is unfortunate. Having explained that descriptions should be short and to the point, he writes:

> Seneca is far from this Method [the use of brevity
> in description]. If he has any Recital to make, tho'
> never so Melancholy and frightful, he begins it with
> such Descriptions as are not only useless, but
> trifling and foolish. (8)

Alexander Pope, as quoted by the indefatigable Joseph Spence, made a similar statement:

> It is a great fault, in descriptive poetry, to describe
> everything. [Spence's footnote: 'That is the fault in
> Thomson's Seasons.'] The good antients (but when I named
> them, I meant Virgil) have no long descriptions:
> commonly not above ten lines, and scarce ever thirty.
> One of the longest in Virgil is when Aeneas is with
> Evander; and that is frequently broke by what Evander
> says. (9)

In this connection it should be remembered what Pope had to say about his own early efforts in penning lines:

> Soft were my numbers; who could take offence,
> While pure Description held the place of Sense.
> Like gentle Fanny's was my flow'ry theme,
> A painted mistress, or a purling stream. (10)

William Warburton agreed with this condemnation of description by commenting on the 319th verse of the imitation of Horace's letter to Augustus:

> Descriptive poetry is the lowest work of a Genius.
> Therefore when Mr. Pope employs himself in it, he
> never fails, as here, to ennoble it with some moral
> stroke or other. (11)

According to Ralph Cohen's The Art of Discrimination Pope really was the main force behind the reaction against description:

> Pope can be looked upon as the traditional voice
> of protest against an undue use of description. He
> opposed "pure description," favored "sense" and
> called description "a feast made up of sauces." (12)

Men of the stature of Pope and Le Bossu were not alone in cautioning against poetic description. They derived close support from a group of theoreticians who are obscure today, but who exerted a certain influence in their own time. James Arbuckle, for example, who was a critic for the Dublin Journal, used expressions similar to those of Lessing, when he emphasized in 1726, the year of the publication of Thomson's Winter, that poetry should work on the emotions and should refrain from lengthy descriptions:

> ... the descriptive part of Poetry, however agree-
> able to a well-informed Imagination, raises none of
> the wonderful Emotions, which are stirred by a
> Recital of those Actions which are attended with
> Dangers, Distresses and Escapes, and the various
> Sentiments which arose [sic] in the Mind on such
> Occasions. (13)

In 1720 the anonymous author of an essay entitled "A Voyage to the Mountains of the Moon under the Equator: or Parnassus Reformed," complained that modern writers used dramatic descriptions purely for their own sake and not to support the story as had done the ancients:

> They [the moderns] have not taken care to make 'em
> of some Use to the Design; but right or wrong,
> with a boyish Wantonness, give us such as are merely
> idle, and not at all necessary ... . When Fancy and
> Chance habe furnish'd them with an Occasion to describe
> a Fountain, a rapid Stream, a stormy Sea, they have
> laid out all their Genius upon it. (14)

These passages show that in the first half of the eighteenth century the concept of ut pictura poesis came under increasing attack, implicitly at least, from various writers who registered reservations against the unlimited use of description in poetry. The most withering statement against poetic description was pronounced by Edmund Burke in A Philosophical Enquiry into the Origin of our Ideas of the Sublime and Beautiful:

> Suppose we were to read a passage to this effect.
> 'The river Danube rises in a moist and mountainous
> soil in the heart of Germany, where winding to and

fro it waters several principalities, until turning
into Austria and leaving the walls of Vienna it passes
into Hungary; there with a vast flood augmented by the
Saave and the Drave it quits Christendom, and rolling
through the barbarous countries which border on
Tartary, it enters by many mouths into the Black sea.'
In this description many things are mentioned, as
mountains, rivers, cities, the sea, &c. But let any-
body examine himself, and see whether he has had
impressed on his imagination any pictures of a river,
mountain, watery soil, Germany, &c. Indeed it is impossible, in the rapidity and quick succession of
words in conversation, to have ideas both of the sound
of the word, and of the thing represented; ... (15)

It is evident that Burke denies words the power to paint pictures in the mind of
the reader. Words are merely the carriers of emotions. Thus, for Burke it is
axiomatic that poetic description is ineffective.

A series of warnings against the use of description in poetry, however,
was not enough to shake the foundations of the ut pictura poesis school that had
grown over such a long period. What was needed was a fully developed aesthetic
theory pointing out the essential differences between poetry, painting, and music.
While Rapin, Le Bossu, Pope, and others were content merely with restraining
poetic description, a handful of aestheticians proceeded to lay down the tenets
that combined to form the basis of such a theory. These elements can be embraced
by the term characteristica, or better ars characteristica. The word, which translates as "theory of signs," was first used in this sense by Baumgarten and Meier.
(16)

3. THE DEVELOPMENT OF AN ARS CHARACTERISTICA

The idea behind the development of an ars characteristica was that the various arts could be easily differentiated once the individual signs that characterize
each art had been definitely established. Such a reduction to the essential elements
would then enable the critics to discuss the nature of the arts, to deal with their
relative merits, and finally to establish an aesthetic hierarchy. Aristotle had been
aware that different principles accounted for the particular effects of each art:

Epic poetry, then, and the poetry of tragic drama,
and moreover, comedy and dithyrambic poetry,
and most flute-playing and harp-playing, these,
speaking generally, may be all said to be "representations of life." But they differ one from
another in three ways: either in using means
generically different or in representing different

objects or in representing objects not in the same
way but in a different manner. For just as by the
use of both colour and form people represent many
objects, making likenesses of them – some having
a knowledge of art and some working empirically
– and just as others use the human voice; so is
it also in the arts which, we have mentioned, they
all make their representations in rhythm and
language and tune, using these means either
separately or in combination. For tune and rhythm
alone are employed in flute-playing and harp-playing
and in any other arts which have a similar function,
as, for example, pipe-playing. Rhythm alone without
tune is employed by dancers in their representations,
for by means of rhythmical gestures they represent
both character and experiences and actions. (17)

Thus, according to Aristotle, painting works with colors and figures, poetry with
language and rhythm, and music with tune and rhythm. The arts, then, differ from
each other, although they all imitate life. Aristotle, however, remained rather
vague and did not develop these thoughts any further.

The next essential differentiation, as has been shown, was made by Leonardo da Vinci. He considered painting a higher form of art than poetry, because
it could capture an object in an instant, whereas the reading of poetry required a
great deal of time. Leonardo thus contributed the idea of the punctum temporis,
or "single moment, " to the developing ars characteristica. Benedetto Varchi
went a step further to conclude that physical objects should be presented by painting while poetry should refrain from description and instead should arouse the
emotions.

The first English critic who came anywhere near to the important findings
of Leonardo and Varchi was, ironically, John Dryden. Although "A Parallel between Painting and Poetry" became the very foundation of ut pictura poesis in
eighteenth century England, it nevertheless did contain the following startling passage:

I must say this to the advantage of painting,
even above tragedy, that what this last represents
in a space of many hours, the former shows us in
one moment. The action, the passion, and the
manners of so many persons as are contained in a
picture are to be discerned at once, in the twinkling
of an eye; at least they would be so, if the sight
could travel over so many different objects all at
once, or the mind could digest them all at the same
instant, or point of time. (18)

Dryden obviously touched here upon the punctum temporis doctrine and like Leonardo conceived of this temporal limitation of painting as an advantage rather than a major obstacle. But he did not pursue this idea any further. He probably failed to realize the importance of his thought. In any case, his adherence to ut pictura poesis would have prevented him from developing a concept so contrary to his main critical tenet.

Anthony Ashley Cooper, Third Earl of Shaftesbury, discussed the punctum temporis and its implications at length in an essay entitled: "A Notion of the Historical Draught or Tablature of the Judgment of Hercules," which was first published in the second edition of the Characteristics in 1714. In this essay Shaftesbury established the principal time-limitation which is imposed on the painter:

> 'Tis evident, that every Master in Painting, when
> he has made a choice of the determinate Date or
> Point of Time, according to which he wou'd represent
> his History, is afterwards debar'd the taking ad-
> vantage from any other Action than what is immediately
> present, and belonging to that single Instant he
> describes. For if he passes the present only for a
> moment, he may as well pass it for many years. And
> by this reckoning he may with as good right repeat the
> same Figure several times over, and in one and the
> same Picture represent Hercules in his Cradle, struggl-
> ing with the Serpents; and the same Hercules of full
> Age, fighting with the Hydra, with Anteus, and with
> Cerberus: which wou'd prove a mere confus'd Heap, or
> Knot of Pieces, and not a single intire Piece of
> Tablature, of the historical kind. (19)

This important passage occurs in the beginning; the remainder of the essay is devoted to helping the painter overcome some of the restrictions of the punctum temporis. The traces of tears on the face of a person full of joy for having found a friend believed lost forever may indicate that person's suffering in the recent past (cf. p. 355). Similarly the future may be suggested through an emblem, such as a lionskin worn by Hercules while still a small boy (Ibid.), or through a difference in the expression of the face as opposed to the "expressions" of the other parts of the body, since one should be aware: "That the Body, which moves much slower than the Mind, is easily out-strip'd by this latter; and that the Mind on a sudden turning itself some new way, the nearer situated and more sprightly parts of the Body (such as the Eyes, and Muscles about the Mouth and Forehead) taking the alarm, and moving in an instant, may leave the heavier and more distant Parts to adjust themselves, and change their Attitude some moments after." (p. 336)

It becomes evident, then, that the best possible moment on the timeline covering a particular action has to be selected by the painter in order to lessen the impact of this major limitation. In the case of the judgment of Hercules, the well-known contest of the goddesses Pleasure and Virtue for the Greek hero's allegiance, the painter's best choice according to Shaftesbury, would be the moment when the troubled Hercules begins to be swayed in favor of Virtue, while still retaining some sympathy for Pleasure.

Shaftesbury's discussion of the punctum temporis constituted the first extended investigation of the temporal limitations of painting and added an important element to the developing ars characteristica; but it seems a little far-fetched when Oskar Walzel declares that Lessing found the core of his aesthetic doctrine here. (20) It is true that Lessing, who read Shaftesbury along with a considerable number of other English authors, accepted the idea that the painter has to choose the most suitable moment of an action for his work, but this did not lead him to Shaftesbury's conclusion that painter and poet essentially have to obey the same laws. He never shared Shaftesbury's argument:

> 'That in a real History-Painter, the same Knowledg [sic] ,
> the same Study, and Views, are requir'd, as in a real
> Poet.' Never can the Poet, whilst he justly holds
> that name, become a Relator, or Historian at large.
> He is allow'd only to describe a single Action; not
> the Actions of a single Man, or People. (21)

Such a statement belongs to the ut pictura poesis school. Shaftesbury's insights into the nature of the temporal limitations of painting were remarkable; but essentially he remained an adherent of the "sister arts."

The first theoretician who actually reduced painting and poetry to their most basic elements and thus created the "signs" that constitute each art was Jean Baptiste (Abbé) Dubos. In his Réflexions critiques sur la poësie et sur la peinture, which appeared in 1719 and which had seven editions by 1770, the Abbé set out to prove that painting is at least as valuable an art as poetry. Indeed, it could be said that painting exerts an even stronger influence on man than does poetry. Dubos supported this idea with two reasons, the second of which was seminal to the development of a theory refuting the validity of ut pictura poesis:

> Je crois que le pouvoir de la Peinture est plus
> grand sur les hommes, que celui de la Poesie, &
> j'appuie mon sentiment sur deux raisons. La première
> est que la Peinture agit sur nous par le moyen du sens
> de la vue. La seconde est que la Peinture n'employe
> pas des signes artificiels, ainsi que le fait la
> Poesie, mais biens des signes naturels. C'est avec
> des signes naturels que la Peinture fait ses imitations. (22)

Painting, then, uses "natural signs," namely colors and figures, whereas poetry depends on words, that is "artifical signs" created by society through convention. Dubos's distinction was to play an important role in eighteenth century aesthetics. Theoreticians first tried to separate the various arts on the basis of this dichotomy. As we will see later, such efforts failed and a successful separation of the arts became possible only when the implications of the punctum temporis were considered. The punctum temporis concept suggested that painting is limited in time, whereas poetry is not. This led to the development of a "coexistent signs-successive signs" dichotomy, a distinction based on the recognition that the colors and figures of a painting exist side by side, whereas the words of a poem follow each other. The substitution of this new distinction for the "natural signs - artifical signs" dichotomy was Lessing's main achievement and it led to his clear differentiation between painting and poetry in the Laokoon.

Nevertheless, the first extended effort aiming at a separation of the arts on the basis of a sound aesthetic theory utilized Dubos's "natural" and "artificial" signs. Dubos, who had affixed the motto ut pictura poesis to his work, did not develop these terms further, but an English aesthetician did, and his work deserves close attention. James Harris's Three Treatises, a rather elaborate aesthetic thesis published in 1744, was the first attempt on the part of an exemplary theoretician to separate the arts unequivocally. "Hermes Harris's" style, known for its lack of imagination, is perhaps more wooden than usual in this work, but his ideas are highly advanced and it is likely that they exercised an essential influence on Lessing.

4. HARRIS AND THE "NATURAL - ARTIFICIAL SIGNS" DICHOTOMY

In Harris's work we find all the elements that in one form or another make up an ars characteristica, designed to categorize the arts. Harris dealt with the punctum temporis, distinguished between "natural" and "artificial" signs, as well as "coexistent" and "successive" signs, ranked the arts according to merit, and finally devoted considerable time to the various possibilities of combining the arts. He also outlined a distinction of the arts based on a "work - energy" dichotomy, an idea that was used by Johann Gottfried Herder in the "Erstes Kritisches Wäldchen," (23) (1769) the first of a series of four critical essays. That Harris did not succeed ultimately was due to the fact that he chose the "natural - artificial signs" dichotomy as the main basis for his argument.

Harris attempted to separate between the arts in the second of his Three Treatises: "A Discourse on Music, Painting, and Poetry." The first treatise: "Concerning Art, a Dialogue," presents a discussion of art in generalized terms and contains among other interesting ideas the concept of a "coexistent - successive signs" dichotomy in embryonic form. The third treatise: "On Happiness, a Dialogue," is irrelevant for this thesis, although it is interesting to note that it is supposed to have influenced Moses Mendelssohn, Lessing's close friend and important forerunner, in his studies on the same subject. (24)

In "A Discourse on Music, Painting, and Poetry" Harris begins by following Aristotle in declaring that the fine arts are essentially mimetic. He then proceeds to explain that music and painting imitate by "natural" signs, whereas poetry uses "significant," or "artificial" ones. In a footnote -- some of Harris's most important ideas have to be unearthed from his abundant notes (25) -- one finds a lucid explanation of these two terms:

A figure painted, or a composition of musical sounds

have always a natural relation to that, of which they
are intended to be the resemblance. But a description
in words has rarely any such natural relation to the
several ideas, of which those words are the symbols.
None therefore understand the description, but those
who speak the language. On the contrary, musical and
picture-imitations are intelligible to all men. (26)

So far Harris has distinguished between painting and music on one hand, and poetry on the other. Painting and music, however, should also be differentiated, and
Harris finds a criterion for such a separation: painting appeals to sight, music to
hearing. Thus his system rests on a combination of the "natural - artificial signs"
dichotomy and the difference in the senses appealed to.

On the surface Harris's distinction among the three fine arts looks rather
impressive. However, close attention to his argument shows that it leads him into
inconsistencies. Harris, for example, surprises with the declaration that poetry
can also imitate through "natural" signs:

Thus, for instance, there is a natural resemblance
between all sorts of harsh and grating sounds. There
is therefore (exclusive of its signification) a
natural relation between the sound of a vile hautboy,
and of that verse in Virgil (Ecl. 3, ver. 27)
'Stridenti miserum stipula disperdere carmen. '
or of that other in Milton (Lycidas)
'Grate on their scrannel pipes of wretched straw. ' (27)

It is obvious that Harris has onomatopoeia and sound symbolism in mind. He tries
to discount the importance of this "natural" aspect of language and emphasizes the
"artificial" one instead, but the inconsistency remains.

A somewhat similar difficulty occurs when Harris, having given a detailed
explanation that language is universal and therefore applicable to all possible
situations and conditions, maintains that painting, nevertheless, surpasses poetry
in its efficacy when dealing with certain objects, such as flowers, fruits, buildings, landscapes, birds, herds, beasts, etc. The reason for this is that painting,
using "natural" signs, is more readily understood than poetry. Its imitation is
more direct and more similar to the imitated object (cf. pp. 77 - 79), a fact
which for Harris was highly desirable. The reader who is content with somewhat
superficial arguments may readily agree with Harris; the more profound student,
however, does not quite comprehend why poetry, if it is really "universal, " cannot describe objects, a rose for example, as well as painting.

Harris's distinctions are most interesting and present an important step in
the development of a school in opposition to ut pictura poesis, but his premises
are essentially incorrect. As has been pointed out by George J. ten Hoor in his
unpublished dissertation on Harris, the differentiation between "natural" and
"artificial" signs is irrelevant, since the signs which form the basis of poetry,
painting, and music are really all "artificial." The cultural environment has a

bearing on our appreciation of even as "natural" an art as music. An Englishman, for instance, usually fails to appreciate Chinese music as fully as an Oriental would. (28) Painting and music, then, are based on convention just as much as poetry is. In all likelihood Harris was inspired by Dubos to use the "natural-artificial signs" dichotomy in his attempt to separate the arts. (29)

Harris could have succeeded in separating the arts unequivocally, if he had paid more attention to the time-element involved; that is, if he had considered the implications of the punctum temporis. He came close to such a consideration in his discussion of why painting excels poetry in the representation of certain objects, pointing out that the poet runs the risk of tedium in his awkward attempts to enumerate all the details of an object:

> -- in as much as painting shews all the minute and
> various concurrent circumstances of the event
> in the same individual point of time, as they
> appear in nature; while poetry is forced to want
> this circumstance of intelligiblity, by being ever
> obliged to enter into some degree of detail -- in
> as much as this detail creates often the dilemma
> of either becoming tedious, to be clear, or if not
> tedious, then obscure .. (p. 78)

Painting, then, succeeds in the representation of appropriate objects such as flowers, fruits, buildings, landscapes, birds, herds, and beasts, not because it is based on "natural" signs, but because it delights the viewer at once, and not only after a considerable time spent in collecting all the cumbersome details into a meaningful whole, as in the case of descriptive poetry. Harris did not comprehend the significance of his own statement; but Lessing did, and he built it up into a doctrine which explains why poetry should leave static description to painting and turn to the emotions, the central issue of the Laokoon. The "natural - artificial signs" dichotomy had to be discarded in favor of the "coexistent - successive signs" dichotomy to ensure a clear, unambiguous separation of the arts.

5. MENDELSSOHN'S INTERPRETATION OF THE "NATURAL - ARTIFICAL SIGNS" DICHOTOMY

Harris's ideas fell on fertile ground in Germany. In 1757 Moses Mendelssohn, grandfather of the famous composer, devoted a lengthy essay entitled "Ueber die Hauptgrundsätze der schönen Künste und Wissenschaften" (30) ("On the Principles of the Fine Arts and the Beautiful Sciences") to the separation and subsequent combination of the various arts. "Schöne Künste" ("fine arts") is used by Mendelssohn as a collective term for painting, sculpture, architecture, and music. Under "schöne Wissenschaften" ("beautiful sciences") he lists poetry and rhetoric. Obviously he is employing the French distinction between "beaux arts and belles lettres."

Mendelssohn begins his study of the arts with the traditional Aristotelian statement that the ultimate goal of the artistic process is the imitation of nature. But it is a modified imitation which he advocates, for Mendelssohn holds that nature has an immeasurable plan, the variety of which reaches from the infinitely small to the infinitely large. Man, on the other hand, finds beauty only in a limited range of size. Also, nature is more interested in aspects other than beauty, so that she often neglects it in favor of some other concern. (31) The artist in his imitation, however, has to single out the aesthetic aspects of nature. A good example for this artistic selection is provided by the Greek sculptures. They present man as a far nobler being than is usually produced by nature. Nature's forms, on the other hand, often tend to be too slim, her heads lack expression:

> Die Figuren der Natur werden von allen Kennern der
> Bildhauerkunst unter die Antiken gesetzt. Die Umrisse
> der Natur sind etwas mager, und ihre Köpfe nicht so
> edel, nicht so ausdrucksvoll, als die Köpfe der Antiken.
> (p. 152)

After this definition of mimesis Mendelssohn goes on to discuss the essence of the individual arts in terms of the signs on which they are based; that is, he does exactly what Harris did in "A Discourse on Music, Painting, and Poetry." Like Harris he works with "natural" and "artificial signs" ("natürliche und willkürliche Zeichen") and he uses rather similar definitions:

> Die Zeichen, vermittelst welcher ein Gegenstand
> ausgedrückt wird, können entweder natürlich oder
> willkürlich sein. Natürlich sind sie, wenn die
> Verbindung des Zeichens mit der bezeichneten Sache
> in den Eigenschaften des Bezeichneten selbst
> begründet ist. Die Leidenschaften sind, vermöge
> ihrer Natur, mit gewissen Bewegungen in den
> Gliedmassen unseres Körpers, so wie mit gewissen
> Tönen und Geberden verknüpft. Wer also eine
> Gemütsbewegung durch die ihr zukommenden Töne,
> Geberden und Bewegungen ausdrückt, der bedient
> sich der natürlichen Zeichen. Hingegen werden die-
> jenigen Zeichen willkürlich [my italics] genannt,
> die vermöge ihrer Natur mit der bezeichneten Sache
> nichts gemein haben, aber doch willkürlich dafür
> angenommen worden sind. Von dieser Art sind die
> artikulierten Töne aller Sprachen, die Buchstaben,
> die hieroglyphischen Zeichen der Alten und einige
> allegorische Bilder, die man mit Recht zu den
> Hieroglyphischen zählen kann. (p. 153)

It is evident that the "natural - artificial" dichotomy corresponds to Mendelssohn's distinction between "fine arts" and "beautiful sciences." Painting, sculpture, architecture, and music imitate nature directly and are thus "natural," whereas poetry and rhetoric become meaningful only through the mediation of convention. Since poetry and rhetoric are "artificial," they can be applied to any conceivable situation and are therefore universal. Mendelssohn leaves no doubt that the poet can indeed express everything:

> Der Dichter kann alles ausdrücken, wovon sich
> unsere Seele einen klaren Begriff machen kann.
> Alle Schönheiten der Natur in Farben, Figuren und
> Tönen, die ganze Herrlichkeit der Schöpfung, der
> Zusammenhang des unermesslichen Weltgebäudes, die
> Rathschlüsse Gottes und seine unendlichen
> Eigenschaften, alle Neigungen und Leidenschaften
> unserer Seele, unsere subtilsten Gedanken,
> Empfindungen und Entschliessungen können der
> poetischen Begeisterung zum Stoffe dienen.
> (p. 154)

It is somewhat astonishing that Mendelssohn, precise thinker as he was, did not modify this claim for universality of poetry. "Alle Schönheiten der Natur in Farben, Figuren," ("All the beauties of nature in color and figure") would seem to be a topic equally interesting for the painter as for the poet, and the expression of the beauties of nature in "Tönen" ("musical sounds") certainly should belong to the domain of the composer and the musician. That Mendelssohn failed to limit the efficacy of poetry in the above statement, a statement that after all occurs in an essay devoted to the separation of the arts, may serve as proof that the ut pictura poesis concept was strong enough to confuse some of its most outspoken opponents.

Mendelssohn's efforts were impeded, of course, by his choice of the "natural - artificial" dichotomy as the basis of his differentiation of the arts. This choice created difficulties that Mendelssohn, like Harris, could not overcome completely. It is not surprising that Mendelssohn had to admit immediately upon having established his separation of "fine arts" and "beautiful sciences" that the arts based on "natural" signs and those based on "artificial" ones do quite often overlap:

> Wir haben zwar das Gebiet der natürlichen Zeichen
> für die Grenzen der schönen Künste, und der
> willkürlichen für die Grenzen der schönen
> Wissenschaften angewiesen. Man muss aber gestehen,
> dass diese Grenzen öfters in einander laufen, ja
> dass sie, vermöge der Regel von der zusammengesetzten
> Schönheit, öfters in einander laufen müssen. (p. 157)

Mendelssohn was forced into this rather embarrassing admission by the onomatopoeic quality of poetry, a quality to which Harris gave his close attention, and by allegorical painting. Mendelssohn is obliged to concede that such atypical forms of art are quite frequent, but adds that a "virtuoso" engages in them at his own peril. Purely onomatopoeic poetry, for example, can attain a ridiculous quality delighting only children, and by the same token the attempts of certain amateur musicians to express concepts that have no natural links with musical sounds have met with scorn:

> Der Dichter bedient sich nicht selten solcher
> Worte und eines solchen Silbenmasses, deren
> natürlicher Schall mit der bezeichneten Sache
> eine Aehnlichkeit hat; und der Künstler sucht
> in den Werken seiner Kunst allegorische Bilder
> anzubringen, deren Bedeutung öfters bloss willkürlich
> ist. Allein der Virtuos muss diese Ausschweifung aus
> einem Gebiete in das andere mit grosser Behutsamkeit
> zu behandeln wissen. Der Dichter, der sich mit
> Vorsatz der nachahmenden Töne befleissigt, ist in
> Gefahr, seinem Gedichte ein läppischen Ansehen zu
> geben, das nur Kindern gefallen kann, und Stümper
> in der Musik haben sich nicht selten lächerlich
> gemacht, wenn sie solche Begriffe haben ausdrücken
> sollen, die mit den Tönen in keiner natürlichen
> Verbindung stehen. (Ibid.)

In the case of allegorical painting the artist has a somewhat wider range. It is quite proper for the painter to follow the poet in expressing certain general truths in terms of individual examples. An abstract idea such as defiance of love can be represented in the form of Diomedes wounding Venus, the tenderness of conjugal love can be symbolized through Hector taking leave of Andromache, and filial love through Aeneas carrying his father through flames and swords. Chance can be suggested by a person with a shaven neck and a braid over the forehead [sic], and silence by a boy putting a finger on his lips (cf. pp. 157 - 158).

The painter, however, has to take care that he is not too obscure. His allegories should not strain the observer's mind. There should be a close link between the painted object and the concept it represents, so that the observer thinks more in terms of the general maxim than the individual "sign" that expresses it. Otherwise a "symbolic," or allegorical sign is far less effective than the most "artificial" words:

> Soll ein Schmetterling die Seele, ein goldenes
> Herz, das auf der Brust einer Person hängt, ein
> gutthätiges Herz, ein gewisser Baum die Weisheit,
> ein Hirsch bald das nagende Gewissen, bald ich weiss
> nicht was bedeuten, so sind dieses bloss symbolische
> Zeichen, und weit weniger anschaulich als die
> willkürlichsten Worte. (p. 159)

In spite of these warnings against onomatopoeic poetry and allegorical painting the fact nevertheless remains that Mendelssohn's separation between the arts is not as clear-cut as could be wished. Lessing certainly found considerable room for improvement in his friend's system. Mendelssohn's greatest fault was that he envisaged the possibility of a combination of painting and poetry. He was greatly interested in combining the arts, a concern that he shared with Harris. According to Mendelssohn the arts could be combined in various ways, whereas Harris held that the only conceivable combination was that of poetry and music. Mendelssohn discussed at length combinations such as poetry with music, poetry with dancing, poetry with dancing and music, and finally painting with poetry, and even painting with architecture and poetry (cf. pp. 160 - 167).

Painting and poetry, according to Mendelssohn, can be fused into a harmonious whole if the artist displays a considerable amount of caution. Only bunglers would resort to the inane device of a cloud escaping from the mouth of a character and inscribed with an elucidating speech. But there are situations in painting in which a verbal explanation is desirable. Often a spectator knows what a figure in a picture represents, but he is ignorant of the occasion that has brought all the figures together. In such a case a short explanation in the form of an inscription of not more than four or five lines is useful. It is obvious that Mendelssohn had allegorical and historical portraits in mind that needed a short commentary for those who had momentarily forgotten their Homer or Ovid. Lessing, of course, would have never accepted such a combination of painting and poetry. Indeed, the very reason of the desirability of an inscription would have been interpreted by him as proof that painting was the wrong art to be used in the particular case, and that the artist should have employed poetry instead. Lessing frowned upon allegorical painting and had little sympathy for historical portraits.

Mendelssohn demonstrated clearly that the "natural - artificial signs" dichotomy, useful as it was in the development of a separation of the arts, had its serious limitations, limitations that could not even be overcome by his great logical gifts. Obviously a different system was needed, an ars characteristica that would result in an unequivocal differentiation of the arts. Ironically, Mendelssohn himself was fully aware of the existence of such a system. He even made use of it, but in too limited a way. What was to lead up to a successful solution was the development of the punctum temporis theory, which, as we have seen above, had been first dealt with at any length by Shaftesbury. The punctum temporis suggests that painting is essentially limited in time, although this limitation can be overcome to an extent by various ingenious devices. Poetry, however, is not subjected to any temporal restrictions. Once this difference between poetry and painting had been recognized as highly important, it became possible to establish a clear separation of the arts which avoided contradictions of the kind discovered in Harris and Mendelssohn, and which entailed significant consequences. But Mendelssohn, in spite of his logic, had not advanced any further than Harris. The "natural - artificial signs" dichotomy still had to be displaced by the "coexistent - successive signs" dichotomy before a valid theory for the separation of the arts could be established.

6. THE "COEXISTENT - SUCCESSIVE SIGNS" DICHOTOMY PREPARES THE GROUND FOR LESSING

It is interesting to know that Harris as well as Mendelssohn touched upon the terms "coexistent" and "successive," but both failed to incorporate them into their system of separating between the arts. The first theoretician in either England or Germany who did recognize the importance of the time element in the differentiation of poetry and painting was a rather obscure Englishman by the name of Hildebrand Jacob. (32) A poet, dramatist, and essayist, Jacob had attained some fame with his poem The Curious Maid (1721), which was frequently imitated. In 1734 he published a little book under the title Of the Sister Arts; an Essay. Critics from the very beginning have allowed this modest work to stand all but unnoticed in some hidden corner on the shelves. (33) There is a possibility, however, that Harris read Jacob, but he did not develop Jacob's essential idea, nor did anyone else before Lessing. Nevertheless, a closer examination of Jacob's thoughts reveals that they were far ahead of their time and rather interesting in the light of the developing opposition to ut pictura poesis.

On the surface Jacob seems to subscribe to "the sister arts" concept as is indicated by his title. The motto that he has chosen, a pronouncement by Cicero, corroborates this impression: "Omnes Artes, quae ad Humanitatem pertinent, habent quoddam commune Vinculum; et quasi cognatione quadam inter se continentur." (34) Jacob's first passage consequently emphasizes the great similarity of poetry, painting, and music:

> If it be allow'd with Cicero that all Arts are
> related, we may safely conclude, that Poetry,
> Painting, and Music are closely ally'd. From
> this near Resemblance to each other they have
> been commonly call'd the Sister Arts, which is
> so great, that it is difficult to discourse upon
> either of them, particularly on the two First,
> without a mutual borrowing of Images, and Terms,
> insomuch that one of these Arts cannot well be
> explain'd, without giving some Insight into the
> other at the same Time. (35)

There follow a few more typical ut pictura poesis paragraphs, and then Jacob suddenly and quite unexpectedly changes his point of view and assumes a language that comes surprisingly close to Lessing's. Admitting that the arts have also "separate beauties" (p. 5) he comments:

> Poetry not only can express the external Signs of
> the Operation of the Mind, which are so lively
> represented by Painting; but also its finest ab-
> stracted Thoughts, and most pathetic Reflections.
> Painting cannot convey its Images in such great

Numbers, and with so quick and unwearied a <u>Succession</u>
[my italics] as Poetry does; and there are almost
innumerable Images in Poetry, which Painting is not
capable of forming, and which are often the greatest
Ornaments in Poetry. (p. 5)

Poetry, then, distinguishes itself from painting by its abstract and emotional possibilities, its temporal aspect, and certain great images that cannot be represented by the painter. These three points form the very principles of Lessing's aesthetic theory as developed in the <u>Laokoon.</u> Jacob elaborates only on the third, the
concept of purely poetic pictures. His respective views coincide with Lessing's
to such an extent that a direct influence suggests itself. This possible influence
will be discussed in Chapter III. Jacob's views concerning the poetic image reveal
that it is characterized by its temporal quality. Thus the basis of Jacob's distinction between poetry and painting appears to be the time element, the temporal
quality of poetry as opposed to the static nature of painting. In other words, Jacob
was aware of the "coexistent - successive signs" dichotomy, although he did not
establish this formula per se, but restricted himself to the use of the term "succession" (of images).

Jacob's curious and abrupt switch in his attitude on <u>ut pictura poesis</u> demonstrates once more the confusion surrounding the concept towards the middle
of the eighteenth century. It seems that Jacob quite inadvertently came across
important insights that were to lead to a separation of the arts, while all along
he really intended to support their close union. But we have already shown that
other theoreticians had grown uneasy and that, notably in Germany, even the
staunchest supporters of "the sisters" were not quite free of contradictions. Indeed one may wonder why not someone long before Lessing had formulated his
theory. It seems that the centuries old concept of <u>ut pictura poesis</u> had such a
strong traditional foundation that critics were reluctant to pursue their own original insights.

Even James Harris, though certainly not a defender of <u>ut pictura poesis</u>,
was limited in his endeavor to chart a new course. Although he tried to establish
the first system that separated the arts, his theory was not flawless for reasons
pointed out above. Harris, however, could have anticipated Lessing's thesis if
he had paid close attention to Jacob's thoughts. That he read Jacob's book cannot
be proved beyond any doubt, but the fact is that in his <u>Three Treatises</u>, published
exactly ten years after <u>Of the Sister Arts; an Essay</u>, he came close to Jacob's
concept of the poetic image, and used the term "succession" to characterize the
quality of poetry.

This key term appears in an important context in the second treatise: "A
Discourse on Music, Painting, and Poetry." Having explained in detail that, although poetry is universal, there are nevertheless situations where painting or
music excel poetry in their imitation of nature, he turns his attention to those
conditions under which poetry definitely outranks its two rival arts. The compli-
cated relations of man and his various actions are largely beyond the spheres of
painting and music, and it is here that poetry is more applicable. These subjects
are naturally of the greatest human significance, since they affect man most

directly, from which it follows that the art that can imitate them best must be the most excellent. (36) Human relations manifest themselves in terms of emotions, sentiments, and manners. Poetry, then, deals primarily with feelings, a point that was later emphasized by Mendelssohn, Lessing, and Burke. In order to feel with the hero an observer has to gain a conception of his character and his circumstances. This obviously requires a sequence of actions. Since painting is extremely restricted in time, a point discussed by Harris in the light of the punctum temporis (cf. p. 63), its efficacy is severely limited. In the case of Aeneas, for example, a painter can portray a man who radiates goodness, but that is all he can do. As to the particular nature and the manifestations of this goodness the spectator is left in the dark. Only poetry can furnish him with further information:

> 'Tis here therefore, that recourse must be had, not
> to painting, but to poetry. So accurate a conception
> of character can be gathered only from a <u>succession</u>
> [my italics] of various, and yet consistent actions;
> a <u>succession</u> enabling us to conjecture what the person
> of the drama will do in the future, from what already
> he has done in the past. Now to such an imitation,
> poetry only is equal; because it is not bounded, like
> painting, to short, and, as it were, instant events,
> but may imitate subjects of any duration whatever.
> (p. 90)

It is regrettable that this keen insight into the nature of poetry did not lead Harris to a revision of his theory. He was too much preoccupied with the "natural - artificial signs" dichotomy to admit any other basis for the separation of the arts. Yet at the same time he was the first theoretician who actually brought up the terms "coexistent" and "successive parts," or signs. But he did this in a different context, namely in the first treatise: "Concerning Art, a Dialogue."

In this treatise Harris is concerned with art in general, a term that is to be interpreted in the widest sense, as has been shown in Chapter I. Harris's aim in this Platonic dialogue is to find a definition of "art" and to describe its refining influence on man. But here he attempts to divide the arts into groups, on the basis of their "end" or purpose. The criterion for such a division is whether an art results in an "energy" or produces a "work." Music, for instance, consists of a tune, which is nothing but released energy, and a dance is the freeing of energy in the form of a sequence of movements. Architecture, on the other hand, results in an edifice, that is to say a work. In Harris's own words:

> Thus a tune and a dance are energies; thus reading
> and sailing are energies; and so is elocution, and
> so is life itself ... Thus a house is a work, a statue
> is a work, and so is a ship, and so is a picture.
> (p. 33)

Now, the crucial point is that each art, regardless of whether it consists of an energy or presents a work, is based on a certain number of "parts" which are grouped according to a certain order. These "parts," or signs, are either "co-existent" or "successive":

> Coexistent ... as in a statue, where arms, legs,
> body and head all subsist together at one indivi-
> dual instant: successive, as in a tune or dance,
> where there is no such co-existence, but where
> some parts are ever passing away, and others are
> ever succeeding them. (Ibid.)

This is the first explicit formulation of the "coexistent - successive signs" dichotomy that I have been able to find in both English and German aesthetic writings. But Harris passes his important discovery over and neglects it in favor of "natural" and "artificial" signs. It is quite possible that Lessing read the Three Treatises and did not overlook Harris's find. This passage, then, would appear to be of the greatest importance in the development of aesthetics. What we know for a fact is that more than two decades after the publication of Harris's work Johann Gottfried Herder, who in the "Erstes Kritisches Wäldchen" set out to refute the Laokoon, tried unsuccessfully to substitute Harris's "energy - work" dichotomy for Lessing's "coexistent" and "successive" signs. Thus we may surmise that both Lessing and his earliest and most forceful critic derived the core of their conflicting theories from the same source.

The first German critic who was aware of "coexistent" and "successive" signs was Mendelssohn, Lessing's close friend and mentor. As has been shown in section 5, Mendelssohn basically differentiated between the arts in terms of "natural" and "artificial" signs, which resulted in the distinction between "fine arts" and "beautiful sciences." Towards the end of "Ueber die Hauptgrundsätze der schönen Künste und Wissenschaften," however, we discover that Mendelssohn also envisaged a closer differentiation of the "fine arts." This differentiation becomes apparent when Mendelssohn discusses the various possibilities of combining the arts, a favorite theme of his. A considerable number of combinations of the fine arts are possible, but there is one stumbling block. Arts which represent "successive beauties" can be combined with those that consist of "coexistent beauties" only with the greatest difficulty, if at all:

> Die schwerste und fast unmögliche Verbindung
> der Künste ist, wenn Künste, welche Schönheiten
> in der Folge neben einander vorstellen, mit
> Künsten, welche Schönheiten in der Folge auf einander
> vorstellen, vereinigt werden sollen. (37)

It is obvious that "Schönheiten in der Folge neben einander" ("coexistent beauties") are identical with Harris's "coexistent parts," whereas "Schönheiten in der Folge auf einander" ("successive beauties") coincide with Harris's "successive parts." Mendelssohn's application of the "coexistent - successive" dichotomy to the fine arts results in two sub-categories consisting of painting, sculpture, and architecture on one hand, and music and dancing on the other. Poetry is conspicuously absent, because together with rhetoric it is listed under "beautiful sciences" and is thus beyond Mendelssohn's immediate interest. The arts belonging to these sub-groups can be united only in an indirect or artificial sense, inasmuch as music in an opera can be made to create a beautiful building and even a whole town, or in-fuse petrified dancers with life:

> Die menschliche Kunst ... kann die Malerei, Bildhauer-
> und Baukunst mit der Musik und Tanzkunst nur uneigent-
> lich, und zwar vermittelst der Verzierungen, vereinigen.
> Man kann nämlich in einer Oper, nach einer bekannten
> Fabel eine ganze Stadt oder ein schönes Gebäude
> durch die Zauberkraft der Harmonie entstehen lassen,
> oder die Tänzer als unbewegliche Bildsäulen hinstellen
> und, durch die Musik nach und nach belebt, ihre ersten
> Empfindungen in freudigen Bewegungen ausdrücken lassen.
> Wer sieht aber nicht, dass diese Verbindungen nicht
> anders als im uneigentlichen Sinne so genannt werden
> können? (p. 167)

Mendelssohn recognizes an interesting exception to the rule that "coexistent" and "successive beauties" cannot be combined directly. Music is quite capable of fusing harmony and melody, the one based on "coexistent," the other on "successive" signs. The reason for this is that the musical sounds making up a harmony are not really arranged side by side in space, but rather blend, so that we perceive them as a single, though combined tone. Such combined tones, of course, can be easily arranged in a melody:

> Wir müssen indessen von diesen allgemeinen Maximen
> eine Ausnahme machen. Die Musik verbindet wirklich
> die Harmonie mit der Melodie, da doch jene die
> Schönheiten in der Folge neben einander, diese aber
> in der Folge auf einander vorstellt. Allein der
> Grund von dieser Ausnahme ist leicht zu finden. Die
> Töne in der Harmonie werden in keinem Raume neben
> einander geordnet, daher fallen sie in einander, und
> wir empfinden nicht mehr als einen einzigen zusammen-
> gesetzten Ton. Dieser kann nun in der Folge nach
> einer schönen Ordnung abwechseln. (Ibid.)

Painting, sculpture, and architecture, however, consist of parts that are "co-existent" in space and hence a union of these arts with a "succesive" one is not possible. Since Mendelssohn does not extend the "coexistent - successive" dicho-tomy to the "beautiful sciences," the combination of painting or even architecture with poetry is perfectly permissible in the form of clarifying inscriptions.

Thus Mendelssohn, like Harris, fell somewhat short of his goal to esta-blish an aesthetic system that clearly separates the arts. His theory was nevertheless further advanced than Harris's because he already assigned great importance to the "coexistent - successive" dichotomy. I believe that Mendelssohn served as a mediator between Harris and Lessing. The former employed only the "natural - artificial" dichotomy in his discussion of the differences between poetry, painting, and music; Lessing eschewed it altogether in favor of "coexistent" and "successive" signs; and Mendelssohn used both systems.

Lessing had yet another precursor who was aware of the essential difference between poetry and painting. Lord Kames's Elements of Criticism appeared in 1762, four years before the Laokoon. In a chapter entitled "Emotions and Passions" Kames discusses the nature and efficacy of "ideal presence," that is imaginary reality. Ideal presence is created in its most impressive form on the stage. The mere reading of a drama will also result in ideal presence, but to a considerably lesser degree. Painting, according to Kames, occupies a middle position. It conjures up an illusion that is more powerful than the one derived from reading, but less efficacious than what the stage provides:

> Of all the means for making an impression of
> ideal presence, theatrical representation is the
> most powerful. That words independent of action
> have the same power in a less degree, every one
> of sensibility must have felt: a good tragedy will
> extort tears in private, though not so forcibly as
> upon the stage. This power belongs also to painting:
> a good historical picture makes a deeper impression
> than can be made by words, though not equal to what
> is made by theatrical action. And as ideal presence
> depends on a lively impression, painting seems to
> possess a middle place betwixt reading and acting:
> in making an impression of ideal presence, it is not
> less superior to the former than inferior to the
> latter. (38)

The important distinction between poetry and painting occurs in the form of a modification of the above statement. Kames recognizes that severe limitations are imposed on painting by the punctum temporis. A painting can give us only one impression that has to be carefully selected from many, while reading and acting exist in time and can carefully build up our passions through reiteration of impressions:

> It must not however be thought, that our passions
> can be raised by painting to such a height as can
> be done by words: of all the successive incidents
> that concur to produce a great event, a picture has
> the choice but of one, because it is confined to a
> single instant of time; and though the impression
> it makes is the deepest that can be made instant-
> aneously, yet seldom can a passion be raised to any

height in an instant, or by a single impression:
it was observed above, that our passions, those
especially of the sympathetic kind, require a
succession [my italics] of impressions; and for
that reason, reading, and still more acting, have
greatly the advantage, by the opportunity of
reiterating impressions without end. (pp. 122 - 123)

Kames offers no new insights into the nature of poetry and painting, but simply
repeats ideas already expressed by Jacob and Harris. Furthermore he seems to
be guilty of an inconsistency, for he holds that "Upon the whole, it is by means
of ideal presence that our passions are excited; ..." (p. 123). Painting is ranked by him higher than the mere reading of drama in its ability to create ideal
presence; thus it should also create greater passions. Therefore, the statement
that reading, nevertheless, can stir up more powerful passions than painting,
appears to be quite contradictory.

Kame's contradiction, however, does not interest us ultimately. What is
relevant is that Kames provided one more voice in the gathering chorus of theoreticians who recognized decisive differences between poetry and painting. Kames
obviously based his observations solely on the "coexistent - successive" dichotomy.
He even used these very terms in his investigation of the effects exerted by "similar" and "dissimilar" emotions on the mind. Similar emotions that are "coexistent"
combine into one emotion that is twice as enjoyable, whereas similar, but "successive" emotions fail to heighten our pleasure. As an example of "coexistent" similar emotions Kames refers to the effects of the various elements that make up a
landscape, such as "vallies" [sic] , hills, trees, etc. The effect can be increased
if other senses come into play. The singing of birds and the fragrance emanating
from flowers can greatly enhance the beauty of the landscape (cf. pp. 161 - 162)

Lessing knew Kames's work, at least in the form of a German translation
by Johann Nikolaus Meinhard, published in 1763, (39) and he, as well as Herder,
considered it an important contribution to aesthetics. Kames, then, may have
fortified Lessing in his conviction that poetry and painting should be distinguished
on the basis of the time element involved, and not by other criteria, such as
Harris's "natural - artificial signs," or his "energy - work" dichotomy.

After a painfully slow process of development that had commenced in the
Renaissance, had been taken up again at the end of the seventeenth century following a hundred years of silence, the stage was finally set in the mid-eighteenth
century for a well-founded theory attacking the ut pictura poesis concept in such
a way that it has never completely recovered. That it was a German who ultimately succeeded, and not an Englishman, while most of the important ideas
leading up to the theory had been developed in England, can possibly be explained
with a quote from Mendelssohn, who pointed out that the English led in originality
and the Germans excelled in methodology:

Unsere Nachbarn, und besonders die Engländer, gehen
uns mit philosophischen Beobachtungen der Natur vor;
wir folgen ihnen mit unseren Vernunftschlüssen auf

dem Fusse nach; und wenn es so fort geht, dass unsere
Nachbarn beobachten und wir erklären, so können wir
hoffen, mit der Zeit eine vollständige Theorie der
Empfindungen zu bekommen, deren Nutzen in den schönen
Wissenschaften gewiss nicht gering sein wird ... Es
wäre zu wünschen, dass die Engländer so fleissig
unsere Philosophie studirten, als wir ihre Beobachtungen
zu Rathe ziehen. (40)

Mendelssohn's concluding and somewhat pedagogical remark, exhorting the English to pay as much attention to the work of the Germans as these in turn were accustomed to pay to theirs, was certainly justified when we consider that not before 1765 can any evidence be found of an English interest in what the Germans were doing in the field of aesthetics. In that year Johann Jacob Winckelmann's epochal work Gedanken über die Nachahmung der griechischen Werke in der Malerei und Bildhauerkunst (1755), the very work that provided Lessing with an issue in the Laokoon, was translated by the well-known Swiss painter Henri Fuseli, under the title of Reflections on the Painting and Sculpture of the Greeks. With the publication of the Laokoon in 1766 the situation gradually began to change. Already in the following year there appeared a short notice on Lessing's work in The Monthly Review; but a genuine English interest in German theory and literature set in only with Samuel Taylor Coleridge.

CHAPTER III

LESSING'S LAOKOON

1. THE PURPOSE OF THE LAOKOON

Gotthold Ephraim Lessing wrote the Laokoon to refute the ut pictura poesis views of a work that dominated the aesthetic scene in Germany for more than half a century and that ushered in the period known in literature and art as "klassisch" ("classical"), a period that had no direct counterpart in England. This work, Johann Jacob Winckelmann's Gedanken über die Nachahmung der griechischen Werke in der Malerei und Bildhauerkunst, mentioned briefly in Chapter II, appeared in 1755 and changed the German idea of beauty, for Winckelmann discovered nothing less than the great aesthetic message hidden in Greek art. "Edle Einfalt und stille Grösse" ("noble simplicity and quiet grandeur") (1) made up the Greek formula for beauty, according to Winckelmann, and this ideal had to replace the artificial pomp of the baroque and the frivolous airiness of the rococo that had dominated art in the seventeenth and eighteenth century on the Continent. Winckelmann was immensely successful in Germany, and for many decades the Germans cultivated an adoration for the Greeks that surpassed the English veneration for the Romans and eclipsed the sterile French classicism which had hitherto dominated German thought.

Lessing, who through Winckelmann's influence had himself become an admirer of the works of the Greeks, nevertheless found fault with Winckelmann for having lumped the arts into one ponderous block, an unwieldy whole that allowed for no differentiation of even the most general kind. Sculpture was Winckelmann's ruling passion, and it led him to elaborate at length on the rules which he abstracted from his observation of Greek statues and which he applied to painting and poetry.

Lessing chose to attack Winckelmann on the basis of his explanation of the composure reflected in the face of the suffering Laocoon. Winckelmann had chosen the sculpture, created by Hagesandros, Polydoros, and Athenodoros of Rhodes around 50 B.C., immortalizing the unfortunate Trojan priest and his sons about to be crushed by the snakes, in order to illustrate the meaning of the Greek ideal of "noble simplicity and quiet grandeur." Lessing in his first chapter of the Laokoon quotes Winckelmann at length and then proceeds to point out his aesthetic error.

Winckelmann held that Laocoon demonstrates "quiet grandeur" by avoiding the piercing shriek of anguish which would be expected of him in his painful situation and which Virgil in the Aeneid has his Laocoön express in all its terrifying force. Instead, the sculptured Laocoon opens his mouth only for a subdued, if anxious sigh. Physical pain and mental fortitude, according to Winckelmann, are diffused throughout the whole statue and find themselves in a state of balance. Although Laocoon suffers, he suffers like the Philoctetes of Sophocles. (2) In other words, such noble endurance causes a spectator to wish he were able to bear misery in this great man's manner. (3)

Lessing agrees with Winckelmann that Laocoon's face does not reflect his torture with the force that one would expect, but he takes exception to the general aesthetic principle Winckelmann was driving at, namely, that control over the emotions characterizes not only the plastic arts of the Greeks, but their poetry as well. Lessing holds the comparison of the suffering sculptured Laocoon with Sophocles's literary Philoctetes to be invalid. A close reading of the play reveals that the unfortunate hero, afflicted with an unhealing snake-bite, had to be banished to Lemnos precisely because with his petrifying groans and shrieking lamentations he disturbed the peace of his Greek fellow-warriors bent on conquering Troy. Homer depicted his heroes as quite susceptible to a realistic expression of pain. Even his gods suffer in a very human manner. Venus, for example, when barely scratched, wails pitifully, and even Mars himself roars with the force of ten thousand raging warriors, when pierced by Diomedes's lance. Thus, Winckelmann's attempt to subsume sculpture and literature under the same Greek concept of ideal beauty was in Lessing's eyes a failure.

The astonishing control displayed by the statue in a moment of extreme anguish had to be seen in a different light. Lessing advanced the <u>punctum temporis</u> theory as an adequate explanation for this phenomenon. The painter and the sculptor, Lessing uses the word "Maler" ("painter") interchangeably for both, are forced to select one moment from the ever changing aspects of nature for their representations. Such a choice has to be made in the most careful manner conceivable, in order to stimulate the imagination of the spectator to enable him to overcome the temporal limitations of the plastic arts. Thus, the most "pregnant" ("fruchtbar") moment of a particular action has to be chosen, a moment that allows the imagination to dwell freely on what precedes the scene depicted and on what may follow. Lessing holds that the very climax of passion is by no means suitable for representation, because the imagination is forced to descend to a far less interesting level on either side of the <u>punctum temporis</u>. A merely sighing Laocoon, for example, stimulates the observer to anticipate with horror his impending extremity of pain, whereas a shrieking Laocoon would impel the imagination to contemplate his preceding groans or his succeeding death, conditions that are considerably less moving:

> Wenn Laokoon also seufzet, so kann ihn die Einbildungs-
> kraft schreien hören; wenn er aber schreiet, so kann
> sie von dieser Vorstellung weder eine Stufe höher,
> noch eine Stufe tiefer steigen, ohne ihn in einem
> leidlichern, folglich uninteressantern Zustande zu
> erblicken. Sie hört ihn erst ächzen, oder sie sieht
> ihn schon tot. (4)

Lessing, then, begins his <u>Laokoon</u> with a highly sophisticated discussion of the <u>punctum temporis</u>, which allows him to challenge Winckelmann's application of a sculptural principle to literature, and which enables him to create a firm basis for his own contention that the arts have to be differentiated. (5)

The <u>Laokoon</u> not only attacks Winckelmann, but also a number of other adherents of the "sister arts," notably Joseph Spence and the Comte de Caylus. Spence is the object of devastating polemic because he maintained in his <u>Polymetis</u> that no subject can be properly called poetic unless it can be represented successfully by painting or sculpture. Such an idea was sheer heresy in the eyes of Lessing:

Von der Aehnlichkeit, welche die Poesie und Malerei
miteinander haben, macht sich Spence die allerselt-
samsten Begriffe. Er glaubet, dass beide Künste
bei den Alten so genau verbunden gewesen, dass sie
bständig Hand in Hand gegangen und der Dichter nie
den Maler, der Maler nie den Dichter aus den Augen
verloren habe. Dass die Poesie die weitere Kunst
ist; dass ihr Schönheiten zu Gebote stehen, welche
die Malerei nicht zu erreichen vermag; dass sie öfters
Ursache haben kann, die unmalerischen Schönheiten den
malerischen vorzuziehen: daran scheinet er gar nicht
gedacht zu haben und ist daher bei dem geringsten
Unterschiede, den er unter den alten Dichtern und
Artisten bemerkt, in einer Verlegenheit, die ihn auf
die wunderlichsten Ausflüchte von der Welt bringt. (6)

The Comte de Caylus fares not much better than Spence for his idea that the Iliad
and the Aeneid should be painted. (7) Lessing was determined to clear up the
chaotic situation into which he believed the theories of the arts had sunk. This
he proposed to do by firmly establishing the limitations of each art. The Laokoon
was designed to relegate the arts to their respective spheres and to refute by
anticipating their arguments any potential adversaries.

2. LESSING'S USE OF ARS CHARACTERISTICA

Lessing gradually builds up his argument that, contrary to the tenets of
ut pictura poesis, differences between painting and poetry do exist, and proceeds
to explain in section XVI of the Laokoon what these differences are. There he
distinguishes sharply between painting and sculpture on one hand and poetry on
the other. As the basis for this differentiation he chooses the "coexistent - successive signs" dichotomy, rather than the "natural - artificial signs" that had been
used by Harris and Mendelssohn.
This choice, coupled with Lessing's logical powers, leads to a differentiation of the arts which is free of the contradictions that marked the attempts of his
predecessors. Lessing establishes the nature of the signs that characterize each
art on the basis of the senses appealed to. Thus, painting uses figures and colors
in space as means, or signs, to imitate, whereas poetry employs articulated
sounds in time. The differentiation of the arts on the basis of the senses, of
course, represents merely a reiteration of what Aristotle had said on the subject.
(8) Lessing's great achievement rests not on his having followed Aristotle's suggestion, but on his emphasis on "space" and "time." Thus, painting is based on
"coexistent" signs ("neben einander geordnete Zeichen"), poetry on "successive"
ones ("auf einander folgende Zeichen"). These signs must stand in a suitable
relationship to what they express. "Coexistent" signs can express only objects
which exist side by side, whereas "successive" signs are applicable solely to

objects which are arranged in a consecutive order:

> Wenn es wahr ist, dass die Malerei zu ihren Nachahmungen
> ganz andere Mittel, oder Zeichen gebrauchet, als die
> Poesie; jene nämlich Figuren und Farben in dem Raume,
> diese aber artikulierte Töne in der Zeit; wenn unstreitig
> die Zeichen ein bequemes Verhältnis zu dem Bezeichneten
> haben müssen: So können neben einander geordnete Zeichen
> auch nur Gegenstände, die neben einander, oder deren
> Teile neben einander existieren, auf einander folgende
> Zeichen aber auch nur Gegenstände ausdrücken, die auf
> einander oder deren Teile auf einander folgen. (p. 115)

Lessing goes a step further to be even more precise. He calls objects
which are coexistent, "bodies" ("Körper"). These "bodies" with their visible
qualities are the appropriate subjects of the graphic arts. On the other hand
successive objects represent "actions" ("Handlungen"), and "actions" are the
proper subject of poetry:

> Gegenstände, die neben einander oder deren Teile
> neben einander existieren, heissen Körper. Folglich
> sind Körper mit ihren sichtbaren Eigenschaften die
> eigentlichen Gegenstände der Malerei. Gegenstände,
> die auf einander, oder deren Teile auf einander
> folgen, heissen überhaupt Handlungen. Folglich
> sind Handlungen der eigentliche Gegenstand der
> Poesie. (Ibid.)

The implications of Lessing's definition are that painting (and sculpture) can
depict only one moment within a sequence that constitutes an action, whereas
poetry can easily comprehend the sequence, but must not linger with any special
moment. Both arts are thus subjected to certain limitations that are a function
of time. These limitations can be overcome to an extent by a skillful artist or
an accomplished poet. For bodies ultimately do not only exist in space, but are
also exposed to time, as is indeed everything in this world, so that in a sense they
are the consequences of actions. By the same token actions cannot exist without
bodies that cause them. Therefore, painting can imitate actions, but only by
implication through bodies, and poetry can imitate bodies, but only by implication
through actions:

> Doch alle Körper existieren nicht allein in dem
> Raume, sondern auch in der Zeit. Sie dauern
> fort, und können in jedem Augenblicke ihrer Dauer
> anders erscheinen, und in andrer Verbindung stehen.
> Jede dieser augenblicklichen Erscheinungen und
> Verbindungen ist die Wirkung einer vorhergehenden,
> und kann die Ursache einer folgenden, und sonach

gleichsam das Zentrum einer Handlung sein. Folglich
kann die Malerei auch Handlungen nachahmen, aber nur
andeutungsweise durch Körper. Auf der andren Seite
können Handlungen nicht für sich selbst bestehen,
sondern müssen gewissen Wesen anhängen. In so fern
nun diese Wesen Körper sind, oder als Körper
betrachtet werden, schildert die Poesie auch Körper,
aber nur andeutungsweise durch Handlungen. (Ibid.)

The practical consequences of this complex interrelationship of time and space
are that the painter has to select the "most pregnant moment" of a sequence of
actions for his representation, and that the poet similarly has to choose the most
impressive quality of the bodies that act as conveyors of the actions constituting
his theme. What Lessing means by the "most pregnant mement" he has ably
demonstrated in his explanation of Laocoon's imperturbable self-control in ad-
versity.

The corresponding stricture on the poet to select only the most suitable
physical aspect of an action, determines Lessing's attitude toward poetic description. Descriptive adjectives should be used sparingly and the enumeration
of physical objects should be restrained. Homer, notes Lessing, was very much
aware of the temporal character of poetry. He describes an object usually only
with one adjective. A ship is sometimes the "black" ship, sometimes the "hollow"
ship, or the "fast" ship, even the "well-rowed" ship, but he is never more precise than this. However, he enters into great detail when discussing all the action
involved in sailing a ship, such as setting sail and arriving, so that it would take
at least five or six paintings to cover it. (9)

If special circumstances force Homer to direct our attention more thoroughly to an individual object, he uses an ingenious method to avoid creating a static
picture. He does this by converting the object into a succession of movements.
Avoiding the description of an object as it appears in its finished state, he chooses
to show how it is being created. If he wants to describe the clothes of Agamemnon,
he relates how the king is dressing:

Will uns Homer zeigen, wie Agamemnon bekleidet
gewesen, so muss sich der König vor unsern Augen
seine völlige Kleidung Stück für Stück umtun;
das weiche Unterkleid, den grossen Mantel, die
schönen Halbstiefeln, den Degen; und so ist er
fertig, und ergreift das Szepter. Wir sehen die
Kleider, indem der Dichter die Handlung des
Bekleidens malet; ein anderer würde die Kleider
bis auf die geringste Franse gemalet haben, und nur
von der Handlung hätten wir nichts zu sehen bekommen.
(p. 118)

Juno's chariot is described in a similar way. Homer avoids a static enumeration
of all the parts that form it. Instead, he has Hebe assemble it carefully piece by

piece, beginning with the wheels and axles, and ending with the reins and cords
(cf. p. 117). In both cases Homer succeeds in changing an object which, as we
know, is based on "coexistent" signs, into an action based on "successive" ones.

Lessing's success in establishing a clear differentiation between painting
and poetry rests, as has been pointed out several times already, on his choice of
the "coexistent - successive signs" dichotomy as the basis for his investigation of
the true nature of the two arts. Unlike Harris and Mendelssohn he did not permit
the rivaling "natural - artificial signs" system to cloud his findings, although he
was fully aware of its existence. Indeed, he found it interesting enough to deal
with it in the form of an amendment to his central statement. In section XVII of
the Laokoon he concedes that the signs of poetry are not only "successive," but
also "artificial." As such they are universal and capable of expressing everything,
including bodies in space. This is precisely what the descriptive poet banks on.
The crux, however, is that descriptive poetry requires too great a mental effort
to please. A poet should not tire a reader out of his wits; he should rather convey
his ideas in such a manner that the reader is unaware of the means that are used.
This is possible only if the poetic language achieves an instantaneous effect. An
elaborate description conspicuously lacks this quality:

> Gesetzt nun also auch, der Dichter führe uns in
> der schönsten Ordnung von einem Teile des Gegen-
> standes zu dem andern; gesetzt, er wisse uns die
> Verbindung dieser Teile auch noch so klar zu machen:
> wieviel Zeit gebraucht er dazu? Was das Auge mit
> einmal übersiehet, zählt er uns merklich langsam
> nach und nach zu, und oft geschieht es, dass
> wir bei dem letzten Zuge den ersten schon wiederum
> vergessen haben. Dennoch sollen wir uns aus diesen
> Zügen ein Ganzes bilden. Dem Auge bleiben die betrach-
> teten Teile beständig gegenwärtig; es kann sie
> abermals und abermals überlaufen: für das Ohr
> hingegen sind die vernommenen Teile verloren, wann
> sie nicht im Gedächtnisse zurückbleiben. Und bleiben
> sie schon da zurück: welche Mühe, welche Anstrengung
> kostet es, ihre Eindrücke alle in eben der Ordnung so
> lebhaft zu erneuren, sie nur mit einer mässigen
> Geschwindigkeit auf einmal zu überdenken, um zu einem
> entwanigen Begriffe des Ganzen zu gelangen! (p. 124)

Lessing, then, bases his argument on the difference of sight and hearing. The eye
grasps an object in an instant; the ear requires a lengthy description. The mind
has to retain all the particulars in order to form in the end a complete image of
the object. If not outright impossible, this is certainly very tedious. Recall at
this point that Harris made a comparable statement when he pointed out in "A Discourse on Music, Painting, and Poetry" that a poet embarking on a detailed description is often forced to become either tedious or obscure. (10) In this connection the Swiss poet Albrecht von Haller comes in for severe criticism. Haller,

according to Lessing, fell precisely into the trap of excessive description in his
well-known poem "Die Alpen," included in his first edition of Gedichte (1732).
Haller described with indefatigable patience a great variety of alpine flowers and
herbs, but Lessing suggests that the reader can hardly imagine the full beauty of
these plants merely on the basis of their poetic description without having seen
them in reality. Haller's method is effective only if the reader is holding the described flower in his hand; otherwise the poetic words say little or nothing. The
laboring poet can be heard in every word, but the object itself remains remote and
cannot be seen (cf. pp. 125 - 126).

Having ended his criticism of Haller, Lessing lucidly sums up his findings.
He does not deny that language is capable of describing a body in terms of its constituent parts, since its signs, namely words, are not only successive, but also
artificial. But this quality of language should be ignored by the poet, because verbal descriptions lack the immediacy which is at the very core of the poetic effect.
They lack the immediacy because the coexistent nature of a body clashes with the
successive characteristics of language. Language makes it possible to dissolve a
body into its components, but its final reconstitution is exceedingly difficult, if not
totally impossible:

Nochmals also: ich spreche nicht der Rede überhaupt
das Vermögen ab, ein körperliches Ganze nach seinen
Teilen zu schildern; sie kann es, weil ihre Zeichen,
ob sie schon auf einander folgen, dennoch willkürliche
Zeichen sind: sondern ich spreche es der Rede als
dem Mittel der Poesie ab, weil dergleichen wörtlichen
Schilderungen der Körper das Täuschende gebricht,
worauf die Poesie vornehmlich gehet; und dieses
Täuschende, sage ich, muss ihnen darum gebrechen, weil
das Koexistierende des Körpers mit dem Konsekutiven
der Rede dabei in Kollision kömmt, und indem jenes
in dieses aufgelöset wird, uns die Zergliederung des
Ganzen in seine Teile zwar erleichtert, aber die
endliche Wiederzusammensetzung dieser Teile in
das Ganze ungemein schwer, und nicht selten
unmöglich gemacht wird. (pp. 126 - 127)

However, in prose, and even in didactic poetry, the extended enumeration
of details is perfectly admissable, because the writer appeals only to the reader's
reason and no poetic effect is intended. Lessing quotes a few lines from Virgil's
Georgics to demonstrate that the Roman poet admirably described a cow suitable
for breeding (cf. p. 127). But in genuine poetry such a description would fail. (11)
Lessing mentions Horace, Pope, and the German Christian Ewald von Kleist as
authorities who discarded descriptive poetry as a barren activity. His choice of
Horace strikes us as rather ironical, considering the role the latter played in
creating the very phrase ut pictura poesis with all its implications. But Lessing is
on hand with a few lines from the Ars poetica which show that the great Roman
poet treated unnecessary descriptions with contempt:

- - - - Lucus et ara Dianae,
Et properantis aquae per amoenos ambitus agros,
Aut flumen Rhenum, aut pluvius describitur arcus. (12)

Of Pope he quotes in a footnote two couplets (13):

That not in Fancy's maze he wander'd long
But stoop'd to Truth, and moraliz'd his song.

and:

- - - - who could take offence,
While pure Description held the place of Sense?

The second couplet, of course, has already been quoted in Chapter II; it is requoted here, because Lessing added a comment by Warburton which he considered an authentic explanation of the poet's own attitude:

He uses PURE equivocally, to signify either chaste
or empty; and has given in this line what he es-
teemed the true Character of descriptive Poetry,
as it is called. A composition, in his opinion,
as absurd as a feast made up of sauces. The use
of a pictoresque [sic] imagination is to brighten
and adorn good sense; so that to employ it only in
Description, is like children delighting in a
prism for the sake of its gaudy colours; which when
frugally managed, and artificially disposed, might
be made to represent and illustrate the noblest
object in nature. (14)

Lessing's ultimate conclusion was that the sphere of painting should be restricted to the description of objects, while poetry should be concerned with actions and the emotions that actions engender. Admittedly, his views of the efficacy of both painting and poetry are somewhat narrow, and Lessing's own limitations, such as his almost total exclusion of music from his consideration of the arts, deserve some closer attention, (15) but he did succeed in creating a systematic theory of the mutually exclusive character of the two arts. It should also be noticed that he did not categorically condemn poetic description, but rather advocated a new definition of the word. The poet may "describe," but only in a dynamic way. He should avoid static pictures and should rather create "progressive paintings" ("progressivische Gemählde"). The "appendix" of the Laokoon contains an interesting list of such "progressive paintings." (16)

By now it should have become obvious that Lessing did not introduce a radically new system to differentiate between the arts. He rather appears to have selected those insights of earlier aestheticians which, put into the proper combination, allowed him to exclude any potential contradictions. Thus, having discovered the importance of the _punctum temporis_ and the "coexistent - successive signs," he refined these technical ideas and applied them properly to refute the _ut pictura poesis_ theory.

3. LESSING'S SOURCES

The questions that arise in connection with Lessing's sources are highly interesting. To what extent was he aware of the work of his predecèssors in England and France? Can one really trace a definite influence extending from England to Germany, or are the various parallels that have been pointed out above merely fortuitous? It is interesting to note in this connection that major German aesthetic critics discount the English influence on the development of German aesthetics. Max Dessoir in his _Geschichte der neueren deutschen Psychologie_, for instance, claims that the German theories can be explained without paying much consideration to England: "... und man kann sogar im Einzelnen nicht immer ausmachen, ob z. B. eine empirische Richtung mehr auf den Pietismus oder auf Locke zurückgeht." (17) Robert Sommer in his _Grundzüge einer Geschichte der deutschen Psychologie und Aesthetik von Wolff - Baumgarten bis Kant - Schiller_ declares that only those elements of English and French thought were used by the Germans that showed the greatest degree of similarity to what originated from their own sources:

> Aus dem englischen und französischen Denken wird
> nur das herausgezogen, was die grösste Verwandtschaft
> zu der aus eigenen Quellen entspringenden Gedankenent-
> wicklung hat. Daher die wunderbare Schnelligkeit, mit
> der die Aufnahme der englischen Gedanken sich vollzieht. (18)

Alfred Baeumler, finally, who wrote one of the best studies of Kant's aesthetic thoughts, substitutes French influence for the English:

> Man hat bisher den Einfluss Englands viel zu stark
> hervorgehoben. Nicht der Spectator, Home und Gerard
> (der Einfluss Burkes war bedeutend, ging aber nach
> anderer Richtung), sondern die Franzosen sind bei
> der Entstehung der deutschen Aesthetik Pate gestanden
> - ... (19)

All these critics have the tendency to trace German aesthetics back to Gottfried Wilhelm Leibniz and his disciple Christian Wolff, who were both under Cartesian influence. While it is true that some of the early German aestheticians, such as Baumgarten, Georg Friedrich Meier, and even Johann Elias Schlegel, one of the two elder Schlegels, chose Descartes and Leibniz as their guides, one can see in the work of Bodmer and Breitinger a very pronounced English influence. The two Swiss critics introduced English literature to the Germanic peoples and made them perceptive for its treasures through their translations of _Paradise Lost_,

Samuel Butler's Hudibras and his Ballads, as well as Pope's Dunciad. They also originated the German moral periodical, modeled on the Spectator. They called this paper Diskurse der Mahlern ("Discourses of the Painters"), and they followed Addison and Steele so closely that they copied from them the ingenious concept of a club, in their case a club of "painters" whose members discussed various issues at length. They also adorned each essay with a Latin motto. The "painters," incidentally, were really poets, who, according to the ut pictura poesis doctrine, were supposed to execute in words that for which their brethren used brush and canvas, namely, detailed descriptions. Bodmer was so aware of his pioneering work in familiarizing the Germans with English literature that he called himself a "useful merchant" [of ideas] .

If anything Lessing was even more interested in English thought and literature than the pair from Zurich. In 1755 he published in collaboration with his friend Mendelssohn an anonymous essay entitled Pope, ein Metaphysiker?, in which Pope's claim to be a true philosopher was questioned. Instead the two authors maintained that Pope's merits were of a purely poetic and literary nature. A few years later Lessing translated Dryden's Essay of Dramatic Poesy in one of his early periodicals, the Theatralische Bibliothek, 1754 - 1759. On February 16, 1759, he wrote the famous "17. Literaturbrief" within the framework of another periodical, Briefe die neueste Literatur betreffend, in which he attacked Johann Christoph Gottsched for his slavish imitation of the French stage and his disastrous influence on the German theater, and in which he suggested that the Germans were far closer to English taste than to French. Lessing also translated Francis Hutcheson's System of Moral Philosophy, and William Law's Serious Call. In addition he planned a translation of Edmund Burke's Enquiry, but never succeeded beyond writing a handful of comments on this work. (20)

The Laokoon is full of references to English poets, dramatists, critics, and aestheticians. We have already mentioned Lessing's stern criticism of Spence's Polymetis, a criticism which pervades the whole book. But he also attacks Addison for the same kind of aesthetic fauxpas, for Addison suggested in his Dialogues on Medals (1702) that the ancient poets imitated the works of sculptors and painters. In the "Materialien zum Laokoon," part of the "Anhang," or "appendix," comprising a multitude of notes and ideas from which he shaped his final version of the book, Lessing demonstrates considerable interest in Alexander Gerard's Essay on Taste, (1759) especially concerning the question of whether sublime objects retain their sublimity when imitated by the painter. Jonathan Richardson's Essay on the Theory of Painting (1719) is mentioned frequently, cited in its French translation as Traité de la peinture. James Thomson, Milton, Dryden, Pope, Garrick, Adam Smith, Hogarth, Chesterfield, and Beaumont and Fletcher are all alluded to. This list is impressive and testifies to Lessing's Anglo-Saxon sympathies.

Unfortunately, he omitted any reference to his most significant precursor, James Harris. Even in his intensive correspondence with Mendelssohn and Christoph Friedrich Nicolai, a bookseller and close member of Lessing's circle of friends in Berlin, Harris was ignored. The three friends discussed in the years 1756 and 1757 major critical and aesthetic problems including those treated in the Laokoon, but the Three Treatises is not mentioned. (21) And yet it is quite probable that Lessing and Mendelssohn were familiar with the work. It was translated by Charles

Batteux into French in 1755, and one year later by Johann Georg Müchler into German. Batteux translated only the first two essays and affixed them to the first volume of a new edition of his Principe de Littérature, which had originally appeared in 1747. It is important to know that the Principe was published not only in Paris, but also in Göttingen. It is also significant that the French aesthetician neglected to give Harris's name. Thus, Mendelssohn and Lessing could have acquainted themselves with the "First" and the "Second Treatise" in the form of this French translation, while remaining ignorant of the authorship. We know that they studied Batteux's writings carefully. But they also were acquainted with Müchler on a personal basis, (22) so that it appears unlikely that they would have overlooked his German rendering of an English theoretician. In my opinion the fact that neither Mendelssohn nor Lessing mentions Harris's name may embarrass the precise scholar, but can hardly be construed as precluding any knowledge on their part of Harris's achievement. Neither aesthetician felt compelled always to cite his sources carefully, and Mendelssohn especially delighted in the use of such imprecise expressions as "nach dem Ausspruche aller Weltweisen" ("according to the judgment of all philosophers") and similar vague phrases. The burden of proof, of course, rests on this writer, and in the absence of any unmistakable evidence he can only emphasize that Harris was the first aesthetician to use the terms "coexistent" and "successive" to differentiate, however sketchily, between the arts, (23) that Mendelssohn was the first German critic to follow him, and that he did so faithfully enough to become entangled in a confusion of "coexistent" and "successive signs" with "natural" and "artificial signs, " a confusion suggested by Harris, whereas Lessing finally cleared up the difficulties and emerged with a convincing conception of the differences of the arts.

The name of Hildebrand Jacob, another aesthetician significant to our study also cannot be found in Lessing's extensive writings. Yet, as we know, Jacob made a highly important distinction in Of the Sister Arts; an Essay (1734) between "poetic" and "pictorial" images, a distinction that was taken up by Lessing and that led him to condemn serial paintings of the kind which Comte de Caylus suggested and Hogarth executed. Jacob recognized the existence of two basic kinds of images, one characterized by space, the other by time. The latter image is beyond the realm of the painter and can be developed only by the poet:

> What Painter can give us the Image, for example,
> which Horace has done in these Words,

>   'Et nova Febrium
> Terris incubuit Cohors. ' (Ode 3, Lib. I)
> This represents a dreadful, active Image to the
> Imagination, and is one of those many, which are
> absolutely out of the Province of the Pencil. (24)

Jacob develops the particular nature of a poetic image still more clearly in his discussion of Venus's appearance to Aeneas in the first book of the Aeneid:

> A great Painter might, perhaps, form a very beautiful

Design from the Description which Virgil gives of Venus,
when she discovers herself to AEneas in the first book
of the AEneid.

> 'Dixit, et avertens rosea cervice refulfit,
> Ambrosiaeque comae divinum vertice odorem
> Spiravere: pedes vestis defluxit ad imos,
> Et vera incessu patuit Dea – '

But to reduce the intire [sic] Image, which these three
or four Verses convey to the Mind, to Light and Shadow,
is impossible. What a Complexity of beautiful Images
are here charm'd up into the Mind, as it were, by the
Magic of a few Words? It is in the brightest Ideas
that Virgil thus represents Transfiguration, if one may
so say, of this Goddess, while she breaks forth from her
Disguise, into the Blaze and Refulgency of Heavenly
Beauty, with all the Ensigns of her Divinity. What a
happy Attitude has the Poet chose [sic] for this
Purpose? With what Grace and Majesty do we behold her
turning from AEneas, and brightning by Degrees into that
glorious Form which confess'd her no less than the Queen
of Love herself? (pp. 5 - 6)

Jacob shows quite clearly that Virgil's image is characterized by action. Venus
is not described statically, but rather as she is slowly assuming her full divine
splendor. The crucial point, of course, is that a painter is incapable of representing such a progression.

Lessing used the same kind of argument to condemn the idea of Comte de
Caylus that an Iliad consisting of a series of paintings should be created. He finds
little difficulty in proving that Caylus's hopes for a Homer of the brush are ill-
founded. The paintings that the count suggests reflect in no way the great poetic
power of Homer. The first paintable scene that Caylus finds in the Iliad, the description of the pestilence raging in the Achean camp, (25) illustrates this failure.
Should Homer have been lost, while a series of paintings inspired by his work had
been preserved, then we could reconstruct the pestilence scene only very imperfectly, perhaps like this:

> Hierauf ergrimmte Apollo und schoss seine Pfeile
> unter das Heer der Griechen. Viele Griechen starben
> und ihre Leichname wurden verbrannt. (26)

Homer's language, however, is full of fire and has a tremendous power. His message far surpasses the factual and sober "account" of the hypothetical painter.
Lessing's comment on the passage in question is almost as sublime as are Homer's
own words, and deserves to be quoted in full:

> So weit das Leben über das Gemälde ist, so weit ist
> der Dichter hier über den Maler. Ergrimmt, mit

Bogen und Köcher, steiget Apollo von den Zinnen des
Olympus. Ich sehe ihn nicht allein herabsteigen,
ich höre ihn. Mit jedem Tritte erklingen die Pfeile
um die Schultern des Zornigen. Er gehet einher
gleich der Nacht. Nun sitzt er gegen den Schiffen
über, und schnellet - fürchterlich erklingt der
silberne Bogen - den ersten Pfeil auf die Maultiere
und Hunde. Sodann fasst er mit dem giftigern
Pfeile die Menschen selbst; und überall lodern
unaufhörlich die Holzstösse mit Leichnamen. - Es
ist unmöglich, die musikalische Malerei, welche die
Worte des Dichters mit hören lassen, in eine andere
Sprache zu übertragen. Es ist eben so unmöglich, sie
aus dem materiellen Gemälde zu vermuten, ob sie schon
nur der allerkleinste Vorzug ist, den das poetische
Gemälde vor selbigem hat. Der Hauptvorzug ist dieser,
dass uns der Dichter zu dem, was das materielle Gemälde
aus ihm zeiget, durch eine ganze Galerie von Gemälden
führet. (pp. 108 - 109)

Lessing leaves little doubt of the painter's failure to capture the immense dynamism of this scene. Not only is he unable to include the musical overtones contained in Homer's verses, but he is also forced to omit the portentous approach
of the enraged god and his deliberate way of proceeding with his act of revenge.
The poet, however, can lead the reader through a whole gallery of pictures.

Obviously, Lessing's argument coincides with Jacob's, but in the true
Germanic fashion he is more precise than the English theoretician, for he introduces two technical terms to capture this important difference between painting
and poetry. Thus, the painter can produce only a "material picture" ("materiel-
les Gemälde"), whereas the poet depicts a "poetic picture" ("poetisches Gemälde"). The contrast between the two concepts is illuminated by a highly significant
footnote in which he contends that the term "picture" ("Gemälde"), though often
used, should really be banned from poetry altogether, since it does suggest a
similarity between poetry and painting which in reality does not exist. He would
have preferred Longinus's term "visions" ("Phantasien"), or better still, the
"poetic visions" ("poetische Phantasien") mentioned by Plutarch, instead of the
ambiguous "pictures" or "images":

Was wir poetische Gemälde nennen, nannten die Alten
Phantasien, wie man sich aus dem Longin erinnern wird.
Und was wir die Illusion, das Täuschende dieser Gemälde
heissen, hiess bei ihnen die Enargie. Daher hatte einer,
wie Plutarchus meldet ... gesagt: 'die poetischen
Phantasien wären, wegen ihrer Enargie, Träume der
Wachenden'; ... Ich wünschte sehr, die neuern Lehrbücher
der Dichtkunst hätten sich dieser Benennung bedient, und
des Wortes Gemälde gänzlich enthalten wollen. Sie würden

uns eine Menge halbwahrer Regeln erspart haben, derer
vornehmster Grund die Uebereinstimmung eines willkürlichen
Namens ist. Poetische Phantasien würde kein Mensch so
leicht den Schranken eines materiellen Gemäldes unterworfen
haben; aber sobald man die Phantasien poetische Gemälde
nannte, so war der Grund zur Verführung gelegt. (p. 112n)

Lessing's ideas concerning description are the logical result of his conception of the basic nature of painting and poetry and go back to his ars characteristica which entails one more demand, the ultimate one, namely that poetry should
deal with the emotions. And in this aspect of the differences between the two arts
we can establish without reasonable doubt an influence on Lessing originating
from a major English aesthetician, namely Burke. Both Burke and Lessing stressed the emotional quality of poetry. Burke emphasized the importance of the elements of obscurity in language. Obscurity suggests mystery which can arouse the
imagination and also invoke the emotion of awe, which is part of the aesthetic
effect of the sublime. Lessing, of course, deduced the importance of the emotions
in poetry from his "coexistent - successive signs" theory. The point is that both
theoreticians deemed fit to peruse the identical three lines in the Iliad to under-
line their contention that poetry should rouse the reader's emotions and protect
him from the disillusioning effect of reason.
Burke, whose A Philosophical Enquiry into the Origin of Our Ideas of the
Sublime and Beautiful appeared in 1757, eight years before the publication of
Laokoon, quotes the Greek text (Iliad, III, ll. 156 - 158) and then adds Pope's
translation. The verses in question describe Helena's beauty in terms of the effect
her appearance had on the Trojan elders:

> They cry'd, no wonder such celestial charms
> For nine long years have set the world in arms;
> What winning graces! what majectic mien!
> She moves a goddess, and she looks a queen. (27)

Burke observes that although the passage lacks the picturesque, or statically descriptive element, it is nevertheless greatly effective and the reader achieves "the
highest possible idea of that fatal beauty." (28) He goes on to say:

> Here is not one word said of the particulars of her
> beauty; no thing which can in the least help us to
> any precise idea of her person; but yet we are much
> more touched by this manner of mentioning her than by
> these long and laboured descriptions of Helen, whether
> handed down by tradition, or formed by fancy, which
> are to be met in some authors. I am sure it affects
> me much more than the minute description which Spenser
> has given of Belphebe; though I own that there are
> parts in that description, as there are in all descrip-
> tions of that excellent writer, extremely fine and poetical. (p. 172)

After quoting six lines from Lucretius to show how an exact description fails to give a valid idea of the object described, Burke precedes Lessing in formulating the important law governing poetry:

> In reality poetry and rhetoric do not succeed in
> exact description so well as painting does; their
> business is to affect rather by sympathy than imi-
> tation; to display rather the effect of things on
> the mind of the speaker, or of others, than to pre-
> sent a clear idea of the things themselves. This is
> their most extensive province, and that in which they
> succeed best. (Ibid.)

Lessing quotes the same three Homeric lines and proceeds with a declaration that comes very near to a paraphrase of Burke's remark:

> Was Homer nicht nach seinen Bestandteilen beschreiben
> konnte, lässt er uns in seiner Wirkung erkennen. Malet
> uns, Dichter, das Wohlgefallen, die Zuneigung, die
> Liebe, das Entzücken, welches die Schönheit verur-
> sachet, und ihr habt die Schönheit selbst gemalet. (29)

Again it seems that Lessing succeeded in expressing the thoughts of an English aesthetician in a more precise, more impressive way. If we take into consideration that he had planned to translate Burke's work, it becomes highly probable that Burke's interpretation of the Helena scene influenced him directly, although there is no formal acknowledgment.

It is my belief that Lessing derived major concepts of his aesthetic system governing the differentiation of the arts from England. Dryden, Shaftesbury, Pope, but especially Jacob, Harris, Burke, and Kames made important discoveries which are all used in Lessing's system and which are synthesized, as it were, into the most complete and most lucid system disposing of ut pictura poesis. If Lessing was not in any way influenced by these thinkers, and in view of his great predilection for English literature this seems hardly possible, then we can at least maintain that in the middle of the eighteenth century a remarkably similar aesthetic atmosphere prevailed in England and Germany. But it is more likely that he did derive major components of his system from England. Mendelssohn probably served as a sort of pacemaker, as I have tried to suggest in the case of the origin of the "coexistent - successive signs, " which can be traced from Harris through Mendelssohn to Lessing.

In comparison with the English aestheticians the French writers seem to have had little to offer Lessing. Dubos is mentioned by him several times, but Dubos did not go beyond the "natural - artificial signs" dichotomy although the credit for having created such a system in the first place certainly goes to him. Furthermore, Dubos's work still used ut pictura poesis as its very motto. The Comte de Caylus definitely interested Lessing, but only in a negative sense, as a whipping boy who deserves to be punished for his inane ideas. Denis Diderot in

"Lettre sur les sourds et muets" (1751) showed an awareness of the restrictions of the punctum temporis on painting, but denied that it constituted a major difference between this art and poetry and music. Those who claimed that different principles applied to these three arts were wrong. Diderot exhorted in this connection Charles Batteux, author of Les beaux-arts réduit à un même principe (1747) to free him from the annoying thinkers who questioned the validity of ut pictura poesis. (30)

The German predecessors of Lessing in the field of aesthetics with the exception of Mendelssohn, who was more a colleague than a predecessor, had little to contribute beyond a certain uneasiness concerning their own uncompromising adherence to "the sister arts." Christian Wolff, Leibniz's popularizer, and Bodmer and Breitinger were interested in the symbolic nature of communication in poetry and painting, and Breitinger even used the term "artificial signs of concepts and images" ("willkührliche Zeichen der Begriffe und Bilder"), (31) but failed to develop an actual ars characteristica. Georg Friedrich Meier, Baumgarten's disciple, did create in his Anfangsgründe aller schönen Wissenschaften a detailed system of signs to account for man's tendency to avail himself of symbols, a tendency which manifests itself in the metaphorical nature of language. But Meier did not extend his ars characteristica to a theory which explained the differences between the arts. (32)

There was, however, one obscure aesthetician by the name of C. F. Brämer who anticipated Lessing, inasmuch as he distinguished relatively clearly between "Begebenheiten" (Lessing's "Handlung" or "Sukzession") and "Dichtungsbild" (Lessing's describing "Koexistenz"):

Denn alle Bilderkünste gehen nur auf zugleich vorhandene
Sachen; und Veränderungen, Begebenheiten und Fabeln
können sie nicht vorstellen, als insoweit sie gewisse
Figuren und Stellungen ausdrücken können, womit gewisse
Bewegungen menschlicher und anderer Körper verknüpft
zu sein pflegen. (33)

This passage comes rather close to Lessing's "coexistent - successive signs" theory, but Brämer ultimately was not concerned with a separation of poetry and painting. He was interested only in pointing out that the former is superior to the latter, although both pretty much achieve the same purposes. Brämer's study, the Gründliche Untersuchung von dem wahren Begriffe der Dichtkunst, was published in 1744, in the very year that witnessed the publication of Harris's Three Treatises.

Mendelssohn, then, was the first German theoretician who applied an extensive ars characteristica to the arts in order to differentiate between them. He did so in Betrachtungen über die Quellen ... der schönen Künste und Wissenschaften (1757), and the revised edition under the title of Hauptgrundsätze der schönen Künste und Wissenschaften (1761), discussed at length in Chapter II. But Mendelssohn can hardly be called Lessing's precursor, since the two met frequently to discuss their various aesthetic problems and were engaged in an extensive correspondence. It seems that Mendelssohn awakened Lessing's interest in these particular problems only to find that Lessing's theory, once it was developed, eclipsed his own.

4. LESSING'S LIMITATIONS

Lessing's theory, commendable as it appears to us in its clarity and logical power, nevertheless suffers from certain shortcomings which in the interest of objectivity should not be allowed to go unnoticed. His most obvious flaw was that he differentiated only between poetry and the plastic arts and practically ignored music. He had actually planned to deal with music and dancing at length in a second part of the Laokoon, but never found the time. For inspiration he could have looked to James Beattie's "Essay on Poetry and Music as They Affect the Mind." Beattie, who published this essay in 1762, but who had formulated his thoughts over a number of years and had read them in a private literary society, held that music should be differentiated from both poetry and painting on the grounds that it is not an imitative art. The efficacy of music rests on the emotions which it causes in the listener and not on any distinct ideas of babbling brooks, peaceful flocks, shepherds, martial actions, desperate escapes from imminent disaster etc. that it is supposed by many critics to raise:

> Music, therefore, is pleasing, not because it is imitative, but because certain melodies and harmonies have an aptitude to raise certain passions, affections, and sentiments in the soul. And, consequently, the pleasures we derive from melody and harmony are seldom or never resolvable into that delight which the human mind receives from the imitation of nature. (34)

Typical for Lessing's regrettable omission of music and his generally somewhat casual procedure was his original intention to entitle the work Hermäa, after Hermes, who among other characteristics was also the god of pathways and coincidence. Thus, Lessing felt tempted to indicate that the contents of the work presented what he had "picked up by the wayside," as it were; in other words, that he did not presume to offer a profound new aesthetic system, but rather some loosely connected ideas. That his work turned out to be anything but rambling can be traced back to his great logical powers and his translucent style, a style which soon was to disappear from German scholarly writing for quite a while.

Although Lessing devoted considerable energy to archeology and theology, he was primarily a man of letters, a critic and dramatist. In the field of the plastic arts he was at best an amateur. Certainly, his ideas concerning painting were too restrictive and too much governed by Winckelmann's preoccupation with classical sculpture. H. Fechner emphasizes that a good many painters and sculptors have achieved fame in direct violation of Lessing's principles by introducing violent motion, great passion, and even the ugly against which both Mendelssohn and

Lessing emphatically had warned. Fechner comments quite sarcastically on Lessing's dictum that the painter ultimately should be concerned with "beautiful bodies in beautiful positions" ("schöne Körper in schönen Stellungen"):

> ... das langweiligste allegorische Gemälde, wofern
> es nur schöne Körper in schönen Stellungen in schöner
> Landschaft zeigt, wäre, ganz im Widerspruch mit
> Lessings Verbot, das Ideal der Malerei; man brauchte
> sich ja gar nicht um die Allegorie zu kümmern, sondern
> könnte im ästhetischen Genuss schwelgen. Eine Aus-
> stellung von weiblichen Modellen oder eine Anzahl
> Nymphen und Göttinnen, von denen sich keine um die
> andere kümmert, würden allen Anforderungen Lessings
> an malerische Schönheit entsprechen. (35)

Lessing could not tear himself loose from the beauty of the classical statue to which Winckelmann had introduced him and his generation. In painting he was so much concerned with the imitation of the human body that he entirely ignored the possibilities of landscape painting. (36) Indeed, in the "appendix" to the Laokoon Lessing jotted down:

> Von den Landschaftsmahlern; ob es ein Ideal in der
> Schönheit der Landschaften gebe. Wird verneinet.
> Daher der geringere Werth der Landschaftsmahler. Die
> Griechen und Italiäner [presumably the Romans] haben
> keine. (37)

Thus, Lessing rejected the painting of landscapes, along with flowers and animals. (38) His full condemnation, however, is reserved for that painter of historical pictures who is interested only in the story itself, and not in the physical beauty of the characters represented, and here he undoubtedly meets with the reader's approval:

> Doch ziehe ich noch immer den Landschaftsmahler
> demjenigen Historienmahler vor, der ohne seine
> Hauptabsicht auf die Schönheit zu richten, nur
> Klumpen Personen mahlt, um seine Geschicklichkeit
> in dem blossen Ausdrucke, und nicht in dem der
> Schönheit untergeordneten Ausdrucke, zu zeigen. (39)

If Lessing's views on painting were limited, so was his appreciation of sculpture. It is somewhat disconcerting to hear that he had never seen the original Laocoön group, which ever since its discovery by Felice de Fredis on his estate on the Esquilin in 1506 had been in Rome. What he saw was merely a plaster fac-simile exhibited in Dresden. It is ironical that up to the time of Winckelmann the marble group had been praised for the violence it depicted. Winckelmann, of course, admired the original during his visit to Rome, but his ideal of Greek

beauty, "noble simplicity and quiet grandeur," obviously prompted him to overlook what did not escape the sharp eyes of a recent critic, namely that: "he [Lao-
koon] draws in air through his slightly opened mouth, draws in his abdomen, thus
pushing up his breast, and throws his back upon the nape of his neck," (40) --
hardly a posture suggestive of mental triumph over excruciating pain. The truth
is that the Laocoön group, beautiful as it is, shows the anguish of human suffering,
an anguish which is reflected in Laocoon's face specifically.

Lessing can also be criticized for having put too much stress on the dramatic qualities of literature and too little on the lyrical element. It is true that
Lessing, the first major dramatist in modern German literature, was far more
interested in drama than in any other literary genre. His "coexistent - successive
signs" dichotomy suggested that literature was characterized by the temporal element, by action, and action is the lifeblood of drama.

Apparently he intended to stress the dramatic character of literature still
more. He planned an amendment to his ars characteristica which was to emphasize
the close link that he saw between his theory of poetry and the stage. A letter to
Friedrich Nicolai, written on May 26, 1769, suggests the form this amendment
would have taken, if Lessing had found the time to incorporate it in the Laokoon.
Referring to a recent critical review of the work by Christian Garve, professor
of philosophy at Leipzig, Lessing admits that he could have been still more spe-
cific in the exposition of his theory, and mentions that a sequel would take care of
all of Garve's reservations. The clarifications would center around the nature of
the signs involved in poetry and painting. It seems that Lessing recognized that
the substitution of the "coexistent - successive signs" for the "natural - artificial"
dichotomy, necessary as it had been to overcome the impasse experienced by
earlier aestheticians, had to be modified. He conceded that the "coexistent signs"
of painting can be both "natural" and "artificial," and added that the same is true
for the "successive signs" of poetry. There is, however, a vital difference between the two arts, namely that painting decreases in perfection in proportion to
an increase in its content of "artificial signs," while the reverse is the case with
poetry. In other words, poetry approaches perfection according to its ability to
transform its "artificial" signs into "natural" ones. (41) Poetry has to lift its
"artificial" signs into "natural" ones and only through this process does it distinguish itself from mere prose. The use of intonation, the position of words, meter,
trophes, metaphors and similar means has an effect in this direction, but only in
drama are the "artificial" signs completely transformed into "natural" ones:

> Die Poesie muss schlechterdings ihre willkürlichen
> Zeichen zu natürlichen zu erheben suchen; und nur dadurch
> unterscheidet sie sich von der Prosa, und wird Poesie.
> Die Mittel, wodurch sie dieses tut, sind der Ton, die
> Worte, die Stellung der Worte, das Silbenmass, Figuren
> und Tropen, Gleichnisse u. s. w. Alle diese Dinge bringen
> die willkürlichen Zeichen den natürlichen näher; aber
> sie machen sie nicht zu natürlichen Zeichen: folglich
> sind alle Gattungen, die sich nur dieser Mittel bedie-
> nen, als die niedern Gattungen der Poesie zu betrachten;

und die höchste Gattung der Poesie ist die, welche die
willkürlichen Zeichen gänzlich zu natürlichen macht.
Das ist aber die dramatische; denn in dieser hören
die Worte auf, willkürliche Zeichen zu sein, und werden
natürliche Zeichen willkürlicher Dinge. Dass die dramatische Poesie die höchste, ja die einzige Poesie ist,
hat schon Aristoteles gesagt, und er gibt der Epopee
nur in so fern die zweite Stelle, als sie grössten Teils
dramatisch ist, oder sein kann. (42)

On the stage, then, the "artificial" signs of language become the "natural" signs
of "artificial" concepts. Thus, drama is the highest form of literature. This passage represents the link between the Laokoon and his other great critical work,
the Hamburgische Dramaturgie, a collection of reviews on the performances of
the "Hamburger Nationaltheater" in the years 1767 - 1768, in which Lessing tried
to raise the taste of the Germans and direct them away from the French to a German theater inspired by the English.

It is possible that Lessing was indebted to Meier for the idea that "artifical
signs" should be transformed into "natural" ones. In the Anfangsgründe Meier had
expressed this thought in the following form:

Je natürlicher die willkürlichen und künstlichen
Zeichen sind, desto schöner sind sie. Diese Regel
ist die Regel der Natur (regula naturae). Alles
gezwungene, weithergesuchte und affectirte in den
Zeichen ist ein Fehler. Nach dieser Regel kan man
viel ungereimtes, in den Titulaturen und Complimenten
der Deutschen, entdecken. (43)

Lessing certainly had his limitations, and the Laokoon presents only a
fragment of the work that he had in mind, but neither before nor after did anyone
succeed in differentiating between poetry and the plastic arts so clearly and unequivocally. We have tried to show that the Laokoon came as the logical conclusion
of a definite trend extending over a considerable length of time. So far the emphasis has been more on the underlying theory of this trend, on the development
of an ars characteristica and Lessing's use of it. But at this point it seems appropriate to examine briefly the more practical implications of Lessing's aesthetic
system.

5. THE PRACTICAL ASPECTS OF THE LAOKOON

On the practical level Lessing wrote the Laokoon to condemn descriptive
poetry as well as allegorical and historical painting, genres which were greatly
aided by ut pictura poesis. The tendency to incorporate an ever increasing number
of static descriptions into poetical works had reached its climax with Thomson's

<u>Seasons</u>, and its imitators. Lessing admired Thomson as a dramatist. In 1751 or 1752 he began with a translation of his <u>Agamemnon</u> and <u>Tancred</u> <u>and</u> <u>Sigismunda</u> which he never completed, (44) and in 1754 he wrote a "Life of Thomson" in the first number of the <u>Theatralische</u> <u>Bibliothek</u>, a critical magazine devoted to drama. (45) But for <u>The</u> <u>Seasons</u> Lessing found only words of disapproval. He referred to the weakness of a good number of modern poets, especially those of the Thomsonian school, who tried to compete with the painter in a field where by definition they had to lose, (46) and in the form of a brief notice in the "appendix" declared roundly: "Leblose Schönheiten um so mehr dem Dichter versagt zu schildern. Verdammung der Thomsonschen Mahlerey." (47)

In the <u>Laokoon</u> proper Lessing quoted at length Ariosto's description of the fay Alcina in <u>Orlando</u> <u>Furioso</u> to demonstrate that the careful enumeration of the most minute details is ineffective when done statically, (48) and praised Virgil for having described Dido as merely "pulcherrima." (49) The contrast between Ariosto's description of the fay and Homer's rendering of the effects of Helena on the Trojan elders, establishes his attitude toward description unmistakably.

Lessing was what could be called an <u>aesthetic</u> <u>purist</u>. The gist of his theory is admirably summed up in a metaphor which he chose from Plutarch and incorporated in the "appendix.":

> Ich behaupte, dass nur das die Bestimmung einer Kunst
> seyn kann, wozu sie einzig und allein geschickt ist,
> und nicht das, was andere Künste eben so gut, wo nicht
> besser können, als sie. Ich finde bey dem Plutarch
> ein Gleichniss, das dieses sehr wohl erläutert. Wer,
> sagt er (<u>de</u> <u>Audit</u>, p. 43, edit. Xyl.), mit dem Schlüssel
> Holz spellen und mit der Axt die Thüren öffnen will,
> verdierbt nicht so wohl beide Werkzeuge, als dass er
> sich selbst des Nutzens beider Werkzeuge beraubt. (50)

It is revealing to know that not only theoreticians like Lessing, Jacob, Harris, and Burke had such puristic tendencies and were aware that literature should be kept free of the influences of painting, especially of static description, but that a number of Augustan novelists indicated that they, like Pope, were somewhat uneasy about the extended use of description in literature.

In <u>Incognita</u> (1690), an interesting forerunner of the genuine novel, William Congreve declared himself incapable of describing the beauty of the heroine adequately and referred the reader to painting. "Incognita" is taking off her mask and is revealing her charms to Aurelian:

> But who can tell the astonishment Aurelian felt?
> He was for a time senseless; admiration had suppress'd
> his speech, and his eyes were entangled in light. In
> short, to be made sensible of his condition, we must
> conceive some idea of what he beheld, which is not to
> be imagined till seen, nor then to be express'd. Now
> see the impertinence and conceitedness of an author,

who will have a fling at a description, which he has
prefaced with an impossibility. One might have seen
something in her composition resembling the formation
of Epicurus his world, as if every atome [sic] of beauty
had concurr'd to unite an excellency. (51) Had that
curious painter lived in her days, he might have avoided
his painful search, when he collected from the choicest
pieces the most choice features, and by a due dis-
position and judicious symmetry of those exquisite
parts, made one whole and perfect Venus. (52)

Congreve goes on to describe Incognita's effect on Aurelian, but eschews stead-
fastly an actual description of her. We are merely told that "her eyes diffus'd
rays comfortable as warmth, and piercing as the light" and that "they would have
worked a passage through the straightest pores, and with a delicious heat, have
play'd about the most obdurate frozen heart, until 'twere melted down to love."
(p. 264) Perhaps the most interesting sentence in the passage is the following
one:

Such majesty and affability were in her looks; so
alluring, yet commanding was her presence, that it
mingled awe with love; kindling a flame which trembled
to aspire. (Ibid.)

This sentence relates to Lessing's principle that poetic description should consist
of the conveying of emotions and not of the tedious enumeration of static particulars.
Indeed, the sentence comes rather close to Lessing's example of Homer's description of Helena's beauty.
Tobias Smollett appears to favor ut pictura poesis, when only his "Pre-
fatory Address to Dr. ..." in The Adventures of Count Fathom (1753) is con-
sulted. The address contains his views on the novel, which he sums up as follows:

A novel is a large diffused picture, comprehending
the characters of life, disposed in different groups,
and exhibited in various attitudes, for the purposes
of an uniform plan, and general occurrence, to which
every individual figure is subservient. But this
plan cannot be executed with propriety, probability,
or success, without a principal personage to attract
the attention, unite the incidents, unwind the clue
of the labyrinth, and at last close the scene, by
virtue of his own importance. (53)

This statement, however, is not very convincing. The first and the second sentence seem to contradict one another, since the former suggests arrested motion,
the latter dynamism. The hero is to "unwind the clue of the labyrinth" and to "close
the scene." But such an active process can hardly be said to take place within the

framework of a picture, which is too static in nature. Therefore, Smollett's figure of speech used to define the novel is not judiciously chosen. Elsewhere, indeed, he demonstrates that he is aware of certain differences between painting and poetry, differences which render painting a better medium for description than poetry. Thus, Smollett feels obliged to present Strap's shock at Roderick Random's revelation of a gambling loss in the following way:

> It would require the pencil of Hogarth to express
> the astonishment and concern of Strap, on hearing
> this piece of news. The bason [sic] in which he was
> preparing the lather for my chin, dropped out of his
> hands, and he remained some time immovable in that
> ludicrous attitude, with his mouth open, and his
> eyes thrust forward considerably beyond their
> station; but remembering my disposition, which was
> touchy and impatient of control, he smothered his
> chagrin, and attempted to recollect himself. (54)

When Roderick surprises his beloved Narcissa in the garden of the country seat where her brother holds her captive to prevent her match with our hero, Smollett again invokes the powers of painting:

> I could no longer restrain the impulse of my passion,
> but, breaking from my concealment, stood before her,
> when she uttered a fearful shriek, and fainted in
> the arms of her companion. I flew towards the
> treasure of my soul, clasped her in my embrace, and,
> with the warmth of my kisses brought her again to
> life. O! that I were endowed with the expression of
> a Raphael, the graces of a Guido, the magic touches
> of a Titian, that I might represent the fond concern,
> the chastened rapture, and ingenuous blush, that
> mingled in her beauteous face when she opened her
> eyes upon me, and pronounced, 'O heavens! is it you?'
> (p. 175)

Smollett, then, could be quite aware of the different roles of poet and painter, and generally limited his descriptions to a minimum. Henry Fielding, on the other hand, indulged in sizeable descriptions. Nevertheless, in Tom Jones we find a passage where he argues with considerable power the case for the application of a reasonable curb on the enumeration of details. Commenting on Tom's sudden outburst of grief over Sophia upon his quitting the inn at Upton in the company of Partridge, he declares:

> We would bestow some pains here in minutely describ-
> ing all the mad pranks which Jones played on this
> occasion, could we be well assured that the reader

would take the same pains in perusing them; but as we
are apprehensive that, after all the labour which we
should employ in painting this scene, the said reader
would be very apt to skip it entirely over, we have
saved ourselves that trouble. To say the truth, we
have, from this reason alone, often done great violence
to the luxuriance of our genius, and have left many
excellent descriptions out of our work which would
otherwise have been in it. And this suspicion, to be
honest, arises, as is generally the case, from our own
wicked heart; for we have, ourselves, been very often
most horridly given to jumping as we have run through
the pages of voluminous historians. (55)

In accordance with these apprehensions Fielding carefully prepares the reader
with a number of allusions to the plastic arts for Sophia's charms before he
launches an actual description of them. This introductory paragraph can be seen
as a veiled admission that sculpture and painting could render greater justice to
the heroine's beauty than mere words:

Reader, perhaps thou hast seen the statue of the
Venus de Medici. Perhaps, too thou has seen the
gallery of beauties at Hampton Court. Thou mayest
remember each bright Churchill of the galaxy, and
all the toasts of the Kit-cat ...
            Yet is it possible, my friend, that thou mayest
have seen all these without being able to form an
exact idea of Sophia; for she did not exactly resemble
any of them. She was most like the picture of Lady
Ranelagh [sic] ; and, I have heard, more still to the
famous Duchess of Mazarine; but most of all she re-
sembled one whose image never can depart from my
breast, and whom, if thou dost remember, thou hast
then, my friend, an adequate idea of Sophia.
            But lest this should not have been thy fortune,
we will endeavour with our utmost skill to describe
this paragon, though we are sensible that our highest
abilities are very inadequate to the task. (pp. 109 - 110)

Mrs. Anne Radcliffe, though given to rather lengthy descriptions, has one
passage in which she suggests that a painter could capture a scene in a more
stimulating way than the novelist. The setting is the burial of Mme. Montoni in
the gloomy castle of Udolpho:

At the moment in which they let down the body into
the earth, the scene was such as only the dark pencil
of a Domenichino, perhaps, could have done justice

to. The fierce features and wild dress of the con-
dottieri bending with their torches over the grave
into which the corpse was descending, were contrasted
by the venerable figure of the monk wrapt in long
black garments, his cowl thrown back from his pale
face, on which the light gleaming strongly showed
the lines of affliction softened by piety, and the
few grey locks which time had spared on his temples:
while beside him stood the softer form of Emily, who
leaned for support upon Annette; her face half averted,
and shaded by a thin veil that fell over her figure;
and her mild and beautiful countenance fixed in grief
so solemn as admitted not of tears, while she thus
saw committed untimely to the earth her last relative
and friend. The gleams thrown between the arches of
the vault, where, here and there, the broken ground
marked the spots in which other bodies had been
recently interred, and the general obscurity beyond,
were circumstances that alone would have led on the
imagination of a spectator to scenes more horrible than
even that which was pictured at the grave of the
misguided and unfortunate Madame Montoni. (56)

The passages quoted above indicate that the age was, at best, uncertain
about the exact nature of the relationship of the arts, particularly of the plastic
arts and poetry, and that the formulation of a clear-cut theory dispelling the confusion was required. This uncertainty about the proper function of each art manifested itself also in the abundance of allegorical, historical, and fictional paintings and the concomitant need to accompany these paintings with a commentary
explaining the intricate action and the symbolic significance. The best examples
for this practice are Hogarth's famous serials. Immediately after the appearance
of his engravings of A Harlot's Progress (1732), A Rake's Progress (1735),
and Marriage-à-la-Mode (1745) numerous descriptions in verse were printed to
ensure that nobody misinterpreted the action or the host of significant details
Hogarth planted everywhere. Probably the best commentary on Hogarth was written in prose by a German professor of physics at the University of Göttingen,
Georg Christoph Lichtenberg. Lichtenberg, who had a keen interest in life in all
its forms, had visited England twice in the years 1770 - 1771, and 1774 - 1775.
He was especially impressed by Hogarth's satiric representations of the English
zest for life and its many and sometimes rather deplorable consequences, and from
1784 until 1796 he wrote his commentaries on Hogarth's sequences in the Göttin-
ger Taschenkalender, one of some 500 literary almanacs and magazines circulat-
ing in Germany in the second half of the eighteenth century. Lichtenberg was read
with great interest; Johann Wolfgang Goethe even wrote in his Tag- und Jahrbuch
in 1795 that he caused a sensation. Undoubtedly the close links that existed between England and Germany under the Hanoverians added to this interest. But much
was due to Lichtenberg's lively style and to his amazing power of perception.

Lichtenberg's commentaries have recently been translated into English by Ines and Gustav Herdan under the title of The World of Hogarth: Lichtenberg's Commentaries on Hogarth's Engravings.

The Herdans affixed a preface to their translation in which, significantly enough, they point out the need for well-written commentaries covering Hogarth's serials:

> And just because Hogarth's themes and the cross-
> section of human life which he chose for their pre-
> sentation were the sort which according to Lessing's
> "Laokoon" theory of the border line between poetry
> and art were not really fit subjects for pictorial
> presentation, they are brought so much the nearer to
> us through the addition of Commentaries like these. (57)

Hogarth, of course, did precisely what Caylus only suggested. He painted stories. Lessing, we remember, discussed in the Laokoon at length why such an endeavor would fail. Lichtenberg implicitly justifies Lessing's position. His keen observations certainly point out details which the ordinary admirer of Hogarth's art would have missed. A short look at his account of A Harlot's Progress may serve as an illustration.

It may not be absolutely necessary to know that Mary Hackabout's father in plate I is a curate with "a wife and ten children living on an income of 150 thalers net," (58) as Lichtenberg confides to us. It may be that the intelligence that the promising girl is "the first of his children to attain by Nature a sort of currency value in the world" (p. 7) is superfluous, although it stands to reason that the good parson will forego the wicked town and be satisfied with a situation in the country, when called upon to provide for one of his younger daughters once Mary's sad fate is known. That the lass hails from Yorkshire, however, carries some weight, since "Yorkshire produces (...) the prettiest girls; ..." (p. 8) and since "... a cart laden with the poorest, though by no means the plainest, of these creatures puts up every week at the Bell Inn in Wood Street, or at least calls there." (Ibid.) This latter fact accounts for the considerable interest the heroine is met with, not only on the part of the rather stately lady, whose patched face should cause suspicion of the gravest sort, and who so warmly receives Mary, but also on the part of the gentleman who stands in the doorway of the inn. Lichtenberg tells us that he is identical with Colonel Charters, a most infamous rogue, inciden-tally known to us from Pope's Moral Essays:

> Giv'n to the Fool, the Mad, the Vain, the Evil,
> To Ward, to Waters, Chatres [sic] , and the Devil. (59)

Lichtenberg's words leave little doubt in our minds concerning Charters's charac-ter:

> The man who stands here with one foot in the court-
> yard and the other still in the doorway, with the

left hand resting on a stick, and the right
engaged in some private business, is the notorious
Colonel Charters. Those who know how readily Hogarth
could hit off a face and figure must be gratified to
see preserved upon this Plate the physiognomy and
form of one of the greatest scoundrels the stylus has
ever rendered immortal. Two of the actors in our
drama die on the gallows, but that man is not one of
them, though he deserved it just as much. He only
escaped hanging because in addition to the numerous
fraudulent practices which lead to the gallows, in
all of which he was a past master, he had been clever
enough to study that one by which the gallows themselves are deprived of their due. (pp. 9 - 10)

It becomes now quite evident that the presence of this gentleman can hardly
be coincidental and that there is a fatal understanding between him and the officious
lady, who is dubbed by Lichtenberg "an old cunning decoy-bird" (p. 13). Indeed,
Charters, "with an income of 60'000 thalers" [sic] , has come "to that dirty hovel
simply to wait for the consignment of girls from Yorkshire." (ibid.) The pro-
curess's name is "Mother Needham," who was granted a place in Pope's Dunciad
(I, 323), and who, as Lichtenberg confidentially tells us, ended on the pillory:

She was arrested, put in the pillory, and on the
second occasion (she was to undergo the operation
three times) was so badly mauled by the rabble on
the maxim: 'I love treason but I hate the traitor, '
that she died before it came to the third ordeal.
This was indeed worse than a hanging. (p.14)

By now the spectator-reader knows that the story can end only in tragedy. When
innocence from the country encounters urbane wickedness, there is but one possible outcome. Just in case that there should be any lingering doubts, Lichtenberg points to an event that may be minor as such, but which in this context assumes
a symbolical meaning ominous indeed. While the good curate is trying to decipher
the address on a letter of introduction "To the Right Reverend Bishop - London,"
his famished steed attempts to feed on the packing straw of some earthen pots and
dishes and manages to overturn the pile, so that the fragile vessels will presently
be so many shattered pieces (cf. p. 7).
From now on the story of Mary Hackabout takes its inevitable course leading to the satirical funeral scene on plate VI. Not the slightest detail escapes
Lichtenberg's attention, so that it can be justly argued that his commentary was
helpful even to the best-informed of Hogarth's contemporaries, who must have
missed a little hint here or there in the great multitude of things crowding upon
the "reader" of Hogarth's pictures. Or did all of Hogarth's contemporaries discover the following minute details in plate II described so artfully by Lichtenberg?
Mary is reprimanding her beau for the slowness of his payments, while her latest

lover steals out of the room:

> 'See, fellow, not so much do I care for you and
> your wretched plunder; a fig for it!', and with a
> snap of her finger she indicates exactly how much
> she thinks of the plunder. It is half a finger
> joint and a little sound that she brings to his
> notice. The right eye has something indescribably
> scornful. But the fellow has money and that is an
> important item which the left eye clearly recognizes.
> The faint is, I think, quite unmistakable. On her
> whole right wing, war is declared, while the left is
> at peace, or at least, some admission is made there of
> guilt. On the right wing the knee is raised at least
> a few hands above the line of modesty, and in an ugly
> way, so that the tip of the foot is turned inwards;
> and the arm is stretched out so that in the Quart [a
> term in fencing] she brings the snap of her fingers as
> close beneath the enemy's nose as if it were a pinch
> of snuff. (p. 18)

There can be little doubt that the modern admirer of the great pictorial
satirist needs the kind of help proffered by Lichtenberg. His commentary permits
us to savor Hogarth's ingenuity to the fullest, and, in a way he turns the two dimensional quality of pictures into the three dimensional one of the drama. To
emphasize the inherent dramatic nature of Hogarth's paintings, Lichtenberg even
introduces dialogue. A very good example is the following exchange between the
Earl of Squanderfield and the rich, but thoroughly middle-class alderman, father
of the prospective bride, in plate I of Marriage-à-la-Mode. The dialogue centers
on the documents entitled "Mortage" which the alderman has his accountant hand
back to the impoverished Earl:

> 'Here, my Lord, take back your estate,' says the
> old man. 'All right!' says the Earl, 'that is
> what your girl brings to our house, and this which
> pulses under here [pointing to the fifth waistcoat
> button], my blood, and here [pointing to the family
> tree] , this cedar of Lebanon, my 700-year-old title,
> these are what my first-born son is bringing into
> your plebeian establishment.' (p. 86)

Lichtenberg had a profound understanding of the nature of Hogarth's art,
and this understanding, combined with an astute perception of life in eighteenth
century England in general, and London in particular, produced a literary work
that should not be overlooked. Certainly Lichtenberg did on the lower level of
social satire what Bodmer, Breitinger, Mendelssohn, and Lessing achieved on
the higher level of epic and dramatic literature, of philosophy, and of aesthetics,

that is, he introduced an important aspect of English life to his German contemporaries.

It would be presumptuous to maintain that Hogarth's delightful, educational, and highly artistic sequences should never have been painted because they disregard the natural restrictions of painting. The world would be poorer indeed, if Hogarth had refrained from painting "stories" and had, instead, concentrated on Lessing's "beautiful bodies." But one can assert without taking undue liberties that Hogarth's paintings, insofar as they represent episodes of an extended action, can be fully enjoyed only after the perusal of a guide similar to Lichtenberg's Commentaries. Certainly, each constituent painting of a series can be separated from the rest and can be admired as a piece of art in its own right. In such a case a commentary is not necessary. The colors and figures arranged by the artist on canvas speak for themselves and their intricate effects are experienced directly and immediately. But Hogarth intended to compose tales. Each painting of a series, therefore, assumes a wider meaning which can be understood only within the context of the whole story. Doubtless, a well-written commentary aids the spectator to grasp Hogarth's complex art in its entirety. Charles Lamb sensed this when he wrote on the nature of Hogarth's painting:

> I was pleased with the reply of a gentleman, who
> being asked which book he esteemd most in his
> library, answered, - 'Shakespeare': being asked
> which he esteemed next best, replied, - 'Hogarth.'
> His graphic representations are indeed books: they
> have the teeming, fruitful, suggestive meaning of
> words. Other pictures we look at, - his prints we
> read. (60)

The Bibliothèque Universelle des Romans, an encyclopedia published in Paris from July 1775 until June 1789, consisting of 224 volumes of about 215 pages each, commenting on 926 works of fiction, includes an entry on the pictorial series of Hogarth, under the heading of "Romans de Spiritualité, de Morale, et de Politique." Although Hogarth's engravings are not reproduced, they are described, and Hogarth is discussed as a satirist. (61) It must be admitted that the method of selection practised by the editors of the Bibliothèque is not completely beyond dispute, since they totally omitted Richardson, Sterne, and Smollett, while devoting 278 pages to The Injur'd Daughter; The History of Miss Maria Beaumont. But their conception of Hogarth as being basically a novelist is ingenious and not totally remote from the truth.

To return to Lessing we note that he reserved his attack on historical or fictional painting for Caylus, most likely because the unfortunate Count had presumed to disparage Lessing's adored Homer by suggesting that the Iliad could be recreated in a succession of paintings. Lessing ignored Hogarth's serials, but what he would have written about them can be gleaned from a note in the "appendix" to the Laokoon concerning so-called "prosaic painters," painters characterized by their failure to adapt the objects of their imitation to the nature of their signs. These painters can be divided into three groups. In the third group are those who practice synesthesia, a method which according to Lessing is not suitable for painting. Significantly Lessing suggests Hogarth as an illustration of this misapplied use of synesthesia:

> Ihre Zeichen [those used by the third group of
> "prosaic" painters] sind sichtbar, welche folglich
> nicht durch das Sichtbare das Sichtbare, sondern das
> Hörbare oder Gegenstände anderer Sinne vorstellen
> wollen. Erläuterung 'the enraged Musician' vom
> Hogarth. (62)

We have attempted to show that Lessing's <u>Laokoon</u> fulfilled a function both on the theoretical and the practical level, and that on both these levels close links can be established between his work and the endeavors of English theoreticians, men of letters, and artists. If nothing else, Lessing clarified the theories of his precursors, thus putting the <u>ut pictura poesis</u> question into a new perspective. What remains to be done is the sketching of the influence of the "Lessing school" on the aestheticians of the later eighteenth century.

CHAPTER IV

POST - LESSING CRITICISM IN THE EIGHTEENTH CENTURY

The Laokoon was not translated into English as speedily as, say, Kames's Elements of Criticism was into German. Indeed, throughout the remainder of the eighteenth century the work was ignored by potential translators, while Lessing's plays received relatively prompt attention. (1) The first Englishman to translate the Laokoon was Thomas De Quincey, who in the years 1826 - 1827 published his version of the work in Nos. XX and XXI of Blackwood's Magazine. His translation was incomplete, but Sydney H. Kenwood maintains that: "it is the noblest English prose in which Lessing's thoughts have ever been clothed." (2) Several authorities claim that the Laokoon was translated in 1767, but this assertion seems to be based on a short notice that appeared in the "Appendix to The Monthly Review, Volume the Thirty - Sixth," under "Catalogue; or, A brief View of some other Foreign Publications." The notice consists of the German title, an English translation of the title, and a short commentary. The German title contains two misspellings, suggesting that the commentator's knowledge of the language was imperfect: Laocoön: oder ueber die grenzen der Mablerey und Poesie, etc. "Ueber" should be spelled with an umlaut, and "painting" in eighteenth century German is "Mahlerey," not "Mablerey." The English translation of the title is correct: Laocoon, or a Treatise concerning the Limits which separate Painting and Poetry. The commentary is vague in its generalized approbation and reveals little other than that Lessing's Fables had left a strong impression on the English. (3)

It appears that Samuel Taylor Coleridge intended not only to write a life of Lessing, but also to translate his collected works. (4) Unfortunately, he accomplished neither. The first complete translation of Laokoon was the one by W. Ross, which appeared in London, under the title of Laokoon, or the Limits of Poetry and Painting in 1836, in other words a full seventy years after the publication of the original.

With this background in mind it is hardly surprising to learn that the first and only eighteenth century aesthetician in England who showed unmistakable evidence of a Lessing influence was the Swiss painter Henry Fuseli, who has been previously mentioned in his capacity as the earliest translator of a major German aesthetic work, Winckelmann's Gedanken über die Nachahmung der griechischen Werke in der Malerei und Bildhauerkunst. (5)

Henry Fuseli, his name was really Hans Heinrich Füssli, was born in Zurich in 1741. Destined by his father for the church, he studied at the Collegium Carolinum under professors Bodmer and Breitinger and became a clergyman after having obtained a Master of Arts. But his clerical career was not to last very long. He took up the cause of a family injured by the unjust action of a magistrate. His complaints to the authorities resulted in the conviction of the corrupt official, whereupon he was advised to venture abroad for a while to escape from any potential retaliatory measures on the part of the magistrate's influential family. He left Zurich in 1763 and after a short stay in Berlin arrived in London at the end of the year. At first Fuseli sustained a modest existence on the basis of his literary pursuits. His most noteworthy achievement as a man of letters at that time was undoubtedly his translation of Winckelmann's important work, an endeavor

which was completed in 1765. His decision to translate Winckelmann into English
was probably prompted by the several examples of excellent translations into German of important English works, set by his old masters Bodmer and Breitinger.
Fuseli evidently resolved to do something comparable in the other direction.

It was Sir Joshua Reynolds who advised him to become a painter. Following this suggestion Fuseli left for Italy in 1770 and stayed there for more than eight
years to study his new profession. He returned to London in early 1779 and two
years later became known through "The Nightmare," a highly original and imagina-
tive painting. But the work that resulted in his permanent fame was the "Milton
Gallery," (1789 - 1799) a collection of more than fifty compositions, forty-seven
of which were presented to the public. (6) He attained the position of a professor
of painting at the Royal Academy of Arts, and in 1805 became its keeper.

In 1801 he delivered his first three lectures of a total of twelve at the Academy. A number of these lectures are of a fragmentary character and of only small
value, but his earlier lectures are of considerable interest. His third performance,
entitled "Invention," is of great significance for comparative aesthetics, because
Lessing's name as the author of Laokoon appeared for the first time in English
critical writing. The reference to Lessing is made only in the form of a footnote
on the first page of the lecture, (7) but the opening passages of Fuseli's argument
are so completely in the spirit of the Laokoon that a detailed analysis is called
for.

Fuseli begins with an assertion that Simonides's famous antithesis "painting is mute poetry, and poetry speaking painting" constituted "no part of the technic
systems of antiquity." (8) Fuseli finds the ancients' disregard for ut pictura poesis
in their "general practice" and in the philosophy of Plutarch who followed Aristotle
in his differentiation between the arts on the basis of the sensuous media involved,
that is, some arts appeal to the ear and others to the eye. These preliminary ideas
are brought into the proper focus by the following sentence:

> Successive action communicated by sounds, and
> time, are the medium of poetry; form displayed
> in space [Fuseli's italics], and momentaneous
> energy, are the element of painting. (ibid.)

Here we have the very essence of Lessing's theory. Fuseli takes care to draw the
practical conclusions from this aesthetic principle, again following closely the
author of the Laokoon:

> As, if these premises be true, the distinct
> representation of continued action is refused
> to an art which cannot express even in a series
> of subjects, but by a supposed mental effort in
> the spectator's mind, the regular succession of
> their moments, it becomes evident, that instead
> of attempting to impress us by the indiscriminate
> usurpation of a principle out of its reach, it
> ought chiefly to rely for its effect on its great

characteristics, space and form, singly or in
apposition. (ibid.)

Fuseli, of course, is interested primarily in painting, not poetry, and interprets
Lessing in this light. One may raise the question, however, why Fuseli himself
did indulge in a piece of "indiscriminate usurpation of a principle," when he painted
the twenty-seven scenes from <u>Paradise Lost</u>. In view of the great beauty of these
famous paintings any doubts raised on theoretical grounds seem irrelevant if not
sacrilegious, but it cannot be denied that there is a discrepancy between Fuseli's
aesthetic theory and his art. It seems that once more we have discovered a contradiction involving the complexities of the <u>ut pictura poesis</u> problem, an aspect
of aesthetics that surely has proved to be extremely fertile for inconsistencies of
all kinds.

Fuseli goes on to extoll the virtues of painting, which he discovers to be
based on the permanent nature of form:

> In forms alone the idea of existence can be
> rendered permanent. Sounds die, words perish
> or become obsolete and obscure, even colours fade,
> forms alone can neither be extinguished nor miscon-
> strued; by application to their standard alone, de-
> scription becomes intelligible and distinct. Thus, the
> effectual idea of corporeal beauty can strictly exist
> only in the plastic arts; for as the notion of beauty
> arises from the pleasure we feel in the harmonious co-
> operation of the various parts of some favourite object
> to one end at once, it implies their immediate co-
> existence in the mass they compose; and, therefore, can
> be distinctly perceived and conveyed to the mind by the
> eye alone; hence the representation of form in figure
> is the <u>physical</u> element of art. (pp. 407 - 408)

Description emerges as the goal of the plastic arts, and description is achieved
through the coexistent parts, or signs, the harmonious arrangement of which
constitutes "corporeal beauty," that is beautiful bodies. These coexistent signs
can be grasped only by the sense of sight in their immediate entirety.

However, the "physical," or static element of the plastic arts does not
satisfy the spectator completely. True aesthetic harmony, according to Fuseli,
is achieved only through the addition of a "moral" element. This "moral" element
is based on action:

> But as bodies exist in time as well as in space; as
> the pleasure arising from the mere symmetry of an
> object is as transient as it is immediate; as harmony
> of parts, if the body be the agent of an internal
> power, depends for its proof on their application,
> it follows, that the exclusive exhibition of inert

and unemployed form, would be a mistake of the medium
for the end, and that character or action is the <u>moral</u>
element of the art. (p. 408)

The "moral" element is introduced into the plastic arts through a judicious selection of the <u>punctum</u> <u>temporis</u> of an action represented by a painting or a sculpture,
in other words through the selection of Lessing's "most pregnant moment":

> Those important moments, then, which exhibit the
> united exertion of form and character in a single
> object, or in participation with collateral beings,
> <u>at</u> <u>once</u>, and which, with equal rapidity and preg-
> nancy, give us a glimpse of the past, and lead our
> eye to what follows, furnish the true materials of
> those technic powers, that select, direct, and fix
> the objects of imitation to their centre. (ibid.)

The selection of the proper moment for the representation of an action requires
"invention," and "invention," of course, is Fuseli's topic in this lecture and is
expounded upon at length.
    Fuseli, then, used the theory contained in the <u>Laokoon</u> almost verbatim to
introduce his main topic. All the important elements are there and, theoretically
at least, Fuseli reached the proper conclusions. Theoretically, because it must
be admitted that in his actual discussion of "invention" he did not eschew rather
obvious inconsistencies between his practical criticism and the theoretical principles expressed in the lecture. Following Lessing so closely, he should have
condemned historical and allegorical painting, or should at least have accounted
for their propriety in the light of the underlying aesthetic theory; in other words,
he should have pointed out where Lessing went wrong. Rather, he chose to praise
Raphael for his invention exhibited in the <u>Cartoons</u>, a series of ten paintings
[Fuseli erroneously refers to thirteen] that celebrate the development of the
Christian religion:

> But the power of Raphael's invention exerts it-
> self chiefly in subjects where the drama, divested
> of epic or allegorical fiction, meets pure history,
> and elevates, invigorates, impresses the pregnant
> moment of a <u>real</u> fact, with character and pathos.
> The summit of these is that magnificent series of
> coloured designs commonly called the Cartoons, so
> well known to you all, part of which we happily
> possess (9); formerly, when complete and united, and
> now in the copies of the tapestry annually exhibited
> in the colonnade of the Vatican, they represent, in
> thirteen compositions, the origin, sanction, economy,
> and progress of the Christian religion. In whatever
> light we consider their invention, as parts of <u>one</u>

> whole relative to each other, or independent each of
> the rest, and as single subjects, there can be scarcely
> named a beauty or a mystery of which the Cartoons fur-
> nish not an instance or a clue; they are poised between
> perspicuity and pregnancy of moment. (p. 428)

This passage is impressive and contains a good deal of truth, but it is hardly com-
patible with the opening paragraphs of the lecture. Fuseli did have a tendency to
be slightly superficial in his arguments and was apt to be carried away by his style
at the expense of the content. In the words of Ralph Wornum:

> His exuberant fancy led him into a circumstantial detail
> of subject and treatment, of style and method, which
> owe their very existence wholly to his own imagina-
> tion. The most characteristic feature of these dis-
> courses, and in which they so materially differ from
> his paintings, is their elaboration of style. If,
> with his ready erudition, Fuseli had as earnestly
> devoted himself to the matter of his subject as he
> has bestowed scrupulous care on the shape in which he
> has presented it, he would have earned a far greater
> claim to our regard. (10)

Nevertheless, Fuseli was aware of the aesthetic trends of the time, and was the
only critic in eighteenth-century England who certainly looked towards Germany
and followed to an extent Mendelssohn's exhortation that the English consult the
Germans who had elaborated on ideas originally derived from England. (11)

There is a remote possibility that Sir Joshua Reynolds was influenced by
Lessing, or at least by some of the ideas represented by his school. However,
no concrete proof can be mustered, and furthermore it appears that Reynolds was
ignorant of the German language. But here and there in his Discourses is a passage that echoes Lessing's ideas. In the "Third Discourse," for example, originally held on December 14, 1770, he implicitly expresses his disapproval of descriptive poetry. Contrasting the "meaner walks of painting" with the "great style" that
is based on beauty, simplicity, and great learning, he draws a comparison between
the lower forms of painting and the less ennobling poetic genres:

> This principle [that the lower forms of painting
> have a certain appeal, but only a limited one] may
> be applied to the Battlepieces of Bourgognone, the
> French Gallantries of Watteau, and even beyond the
> exhibition of animal life, to the Landscapes of
> Claude Lorraine, and the Sea-Views of Vandervelde.
> All these painters have, in general, the same right,
> in different degrees, to the name of a painter, which
> a satirist, an epigrammatist, a sonneteer, a writer
> of pastorals, or descriptive poetry, has to that of a poet. (12)

In the "Fourth Discourse" Reynolds touches on the punctum temporis and the temporal restrictions under which painting labors in contrast to the freedom enjoyed by poetry:

> A Painter must compensate the natural deficiencies
> of his art. He has but one sentence to utter, but
> one moment to exhibit. He cannot, like the poet or
> historian, expatiate, and impress the mind with
> great veneration for the character of the hero or
> saint he represents, though he lets us know, at the
> same time that the saint was deformed, or the hero
> lame. The painter has no other means of giving an
> idea of the dignity of the mind, but by that external
> appearance which grandeur of thought does generally,
> though not always, impress on the countenance; and
> by that correspondence of figure to sentiment and
> situation, which all men wish, but cannot command.
> (p. 348)

In the "Tenth Discourse" Reynolds even finds differences between painting and sculpture, differences that Lessing completely ignored:

> Though Painting and Sculpture are, like many other
> arts, governed by the same general principles, yet in
> the detail, or what may be called the by-laws of each
> art, there seems to be no longer any connection be-
> tween them. The different materials upon which those
> two arts exert their powers, must infallibly create a
> proportional difference in their practice. There are
> many petty excellencies which the Painter attains with
> ease, but which are impracticable in Sculpture;
> and which, even if it could accomplish them, would
> add nothing to the true value and dignity of the
> work. (II, p. 13)

Thus, the sculptor of "The Apostles" in the church of St. John Lateran incurs Reynolds's censure for having imitated the practice of painters to enhance the majesty of a figure by disposing the drapery in great quantity. In sculpture the heavy nature of the stone belies the light and airy appearance of the flowing dra- pery and prevents it from exerting the desired effect on the spectator (cf. II, p. 16). Similarly, the attempt of a sculptor to place his figures in a bas-relief on different planes, some in the foreground and others more in the background like an historical painting fails, because the sculptor can suggest the difference in distance only by diminishing the dimensions of those figures supposed to be further away and by "relieving" them less from the surface, a procedure that defies its purpose, since in the end all figures, large or small, invariably appear to be at the same distance from the eye of the beholder anyway (cf. ibid.).

Reynolds, however, is not consistent in his stand against ut pictura poesis. In the "Seventh Discourse," for example, he counsels his students to improve their artistic resources by reading:

> Every man whose business is description, ought to
> be tolerably conversant with the poets, in some
> language or other; that he may imbibe a poetical
> spirit, and enlarge his stock of ideas. He ought
> to acquire an habit of comparing and digesting his
> notions. He ought not to be wholly unacquainted with
> that part of philosophy which gives an insight into
> human nature, and relates to the manners, characters,
> passions, and affections. (I, p. 407)

Lessing conceivably could have gone along with this idea, although he would have pointed out that the poet's and the painter's "description" differ remarkably in quality. But Reynolds's ideas concerning allegorical painting are totally opposed to Lessing's strict interpretation of the differences of the arts:

> What has been so often said to the disadvantage of
> allegorical poetry, – that it is tedious, and
> uninteresting, – cannot with the same porpriety be
> applied to painting, where the interest is of a
> different kind. If allegorical painting produces a
> greater variety of ideal beauty, a richer, a more
> various and delightful composition, and gives to the
> artist a greater opportunity of exhibiting his skill,
> all the interest he wishes for is accomplished;
> such a picture not only attracts, but fixes the
> attention. (I, pp. 420 – 421)

In the same discourse he finally appears as an almost unqualified adherent of the "sister arts" concept when he writes:

> It is by the analogy that one art bears to another,
> that many things are ascertained, which either
> were but faintly seen, or, perhaps, would not have
> been discovered at all, if the inventor had not
> received the first hints from the practices of a
> sister art on a similar occasion. The frequent
> allusions which every man who treats of any art
> is obliged to make to others, in order to illus-
> trate and confirm his principles, sufficiently
> show their near connection and inseparable relation.
> (I, p. 426)

This last paragraph ties in with Reynolds's incorporation into his collected works of Du Fresnoy's De arte graphica in the form of the Latin original and an English translation by William Mason, to which Reynolds added various annotations, and Dryden's "Parallel between Poetry and Painting." With Reynolds, then, we have no clear-cut advancement concerning the question of ut pictura poesis, as compared to such a theoretician as Shaftesbury. He rather appears to be an imitator of the philosophical earl, than a conscientious student of Lessing or Harris.

A careful examination of the Lectures on Rhetoric and Belles Lettres composed by Hugh Blair in twenty-four years (1759 - 1783) results in the same impression of unevenness. In "Lecture V," written around 1760, Blair applies the "natural - artificial signs" distinction to differentiate between the plastic arts and poetry. He does this in terms of "imitation" and "description":

> Neither discourse in general, nor poetry in parti-
> cular, can be called altogether imitative arts.
> We must distinguish betwixt imitation and descrip-
> tion, which are ideas that should not be confounded.
> Imitation is performed by means of somewhat that has
> [sic] a natural likeness and resemblance to the thing
> imitated, and of consequence is understood by all;
> such are statues and pictures. Description, again,
> is the raising in the mind the conception of an object
> by means of some arbitrary or instituted symbols,
> understood only by those who agree in the institution
> of them; such are words and writing. Words have no
> natural resemblance to the ideas or objects which
> they are employed to signify; but a statue or a
> picture has a natural likeness to the original: and,
> therefore, imitation and description differ consider-
> ably, in their nature, from each other. (13)

Now, poetry can also be imitative in certain ways. Dialogue, for example, should properly be called "imitative," whereas the description of a storm such as Virgil's rendering of the tempest in the first book of the Aeneid can hardly be understood as a close copy of nature. Blair adds a highly significant footnote to the question of the exact nature of poetry. Maintaining that, regardless of whether poetry is more descriptive or more imitative, it excells over the other arts, he refers to Harris's Three Treatises:

> How far either the imitation or the description
> which poetry employs is superior to the imitative
> powers of painting and music, is well shown by
> Mr. Harris, in his Treatise on Music, Painting,
> and Poetry. The chief advantage which poetry, or
> discourse in general, enjoys, is that whereas, by
> the nature of his art, the painter is confined to
> the representation of a single moment, writing and
> discourse can trace a transaction through its whole

progress. That moment, indeed, which the painter
pitches upon for the subject of his picture, he
may be said to exhibit with more advantage than the
poet or the orator; inasmuch as he sets before us,
in one view, all the minute concurrent circumstances
of the event which happens in one individual point
of time, as they appear in nature; while discourse
is obliged to exhibit them in succession, and by
means of a detail, which is in danger of becoming
tedious, in order to be clear, or if not tedious, is
in danger of being obscure. But to that point of
time which he has chosen, the painter being entirely
confined, he cannot exhibit various stages of the same
action or event; and he is subject to this further
defect, that he can only exhibit objects as they appear
to the eye, and can very imperfectly delineate characters and sentiments, which are the noblest subjects
of imitation or description. The power of representing these, with full advantage, gives a high superiority
to discourse and writing above all other imitative arts.
(pp. 61n - 62n.)

In this footnote Blair, as it were, sums up the major findings of Harris,
findings, which as we have seen, came close to the theory of the Laokoon, without however reaching Lessing's impressive perspicuity. Thus, in the fifth lecture
Blair recognizes not only the "natural - artificial signs" dichotomy, but also the
punctum temporis theory and its implication, the "coexistent" nature of the plastic
arts, and the "successive" character of poetry. The use of the term "description"
to define the main efficacy of poetry is, of course, misleading and clouds his findings considerably. It is possible that this confusion of terms caused him to execute
in the thirty-ninth and fortieth lectures a rather radical about-face. Praising "description" in the sense of an enumeration of details as desirable, he abruptly establishes a sharp contradiction to his earlier warnings against the tedium that such
descriptions could cause. Drawing parallels between poetry and painting Blair apparently became a full-fledged ut pictura poesis man in his later years. In "Lecture XXXIX, " for example, he praises pastoral poetry for the wide range of descriptions it offers the poet:

At the same time, no subject seems to be more
favorable to poetry. Amidst rural objects, nature
presents, on all hands, the finest field for description; and nothing appears to flow more, of its
own accord, into poetical numbers, than rivers
and mountains, meadows and hills, flocks and trees,
and shepherds void of care. Hence this species of
poetry has, at all times, allured many readers, and
excited many writers. (pp. 326 - 327)

As if this were not enough, Blair offers detailed advice covering the exact nature of pastoral description:

> In every pastoral, a scene, or rural prospect, should
> be distinctly drawn, and set before us. It is not
> enough, that we have those unmeaning groups of violets
> and roses, of birds, and brooks, and breezes, which
> our common pastoral-mongers throw together, and
> which are perpetually recurring upon us without varia-
> tion. A good poet ought to give us such a landscape,
> as a painter could copy after. His objects must be
> particularized; the stream, the rock, or the tree,
> must each of them stand forth, so as to make a figure
> in the imagination, and to give us a pleasing concep-
> tion of the place where we are. (p. 529)

Thus, the ultimate criterion of a good pastoral poet is the ease with which a painter can copy his scenes. Description, then, emerges as the very cornerstone of poetry, an impression which is supported by Blair's view on descriptive poetry in "Lecture XL":

> Description is the great test of a poet's imagina-
> tion; and always distinguishes an original from a
> second-rate genius. To a writer of the inferior
> class, nature, when at any time he attempts to de-
> scribe it, appears exhausted by those who have gone
> before him in the same track. He sees nothing new,
> or peculiar, in the object which he would paint; his
> conceptions of it are loose and vague; and his expres-
> sions, of course, feeble and general. He gives us
> words rather than ideas; we meet with the language
> indeed of poetical description, but we apprehend the
> object described very indistinctly. Whereas, a true
> poet makes us imagine that we see it before our eyes;
> he catches the distinguishing features; he gives it
> the colours of life and reality; he places it in such
> a light that a painter could copy after him. (pp. 548 -
> 549)

Blair, at this point, retains only one faint touch of an awareness that poetry, perhaps, should not completely be equated with painting, for he emphasizes the advantages of "brevity" in description: "Brevity, almost always, contributes to vivacity." (p. 549) He proves this interesting argument by quoting Thomson's description of the plague that befell the fleet of Admiral Vernon at Carthagena in his "Summer":

> ' - - - you, gallant Vernon, saw

The miserable scene; you pitying saw
To infant weakness sunk the warrior's arms;
Saw the deep-racking pang; the ghastly form;
The lip pale quiv'ring; and the beamless eye
No more with ardour bright; you heard the groans
Of agonizing ships from shore to shore;
Heard nightly plunged, amid the sullen waves,
The frequent corse.' (14)

Blair discovers "brevity" used to the best advantage in the last two lines of this quotation:

All the circumstances here are properly chosen,
for setting this dismal scene in a strong light
before our eyes. But what is most striking in the
picture is the last image. We are conducted through
all the scenes of distress, till we come to the
mortality prevailing in the fleet, which a vulgar
poet would have described by exaggerated expressions,
concerning the multiplied trophies and victories of
death. But, how much more is the imagination impressed
by this single circumstance, of dead bodies thrown over-
board every night; of the constant sound of their falling
into the waters; and of the admiral listening
to this melancholy sound, so often striking his ear!
                'Heard nightly plunged, amid the sullen waves,
                The frequent corse.' (p. 550)

This passage is reminiscent of Rapin's, Le Bossu's, and Pope's emphasis on short descriptions, and even contains an echo of sorts of Lessing's praise for Homer's active depictions, but, on the whole, the impression remains that Blair sometime during his long career had abandoned an earlier interest in the differences between the arts in favor of a rather traditional endorsement of the ut pictura poesis concept. This impression is corroborated by the close parallel between poetry and music that he draws in his discussion of the nature of the ode in "Lecture XXXIX." (15)

It is somewhat surprising that Blair dismissed his former interest in Harris's work, without following it up by a thorough study of Laokoon, surprising, because elsewhere he gives evidence of a keen interest in German works. Among the contemporary poets of pastorals, for instance, he assigns the palm to the Swiss poet Salomon Gessner: (16)

Of all the moderns, M. Gesner [sic], a poet of
Switzerland, has been the most successful in his
pastoral compositions. He has introduced into
his Idylls (as he entitles them) many new ideas.
His rural scenery is often striking, and his de-

scriptions are lively. He presents pastoral life to
us, with all the embellishments of which it is susceptible; but without any excess of refinement.
What forms the chief merit of this poet, is that he
writes to the heart; and has enriched the subjects
of his Idylls with incidents which give rise to much
tender sentiment. Scenes of domestic felicity are
beautifully painted. The mutual affection of husbands
and wives, of parents and children, of brothers and
sisters, as well as lovers, are displayed in a pleasing
and touching manner. (p. 534)

This thorough analysis of Gessner seems to suggest Blair's profound familiarity
with the German language, but the next sentence disappoints us in our expectation
and provides the key for his disinterest in Lessing: "From not understanding the
language in which M. Gesner writes, I can be no judge of the poetry of his style:
but, in the subject and conduct of his pastorals, he appears to me to have outdone
all the moderns." (pp. 534 - 535) With this statement the very crux of the problem of German influence on eighteenth century English aesthetics has been reached. The simple fact is that apparently no aesthetician, with the sole exception of
Fuseli, could read German. The educated English gentlemen were well-versed in
Latin, and perhaps even Greek. Some spoke French, a language cultivated particularly by the ladies of fashion in their drawing rooms, and a small minority knew
some words in Italian. But German was generally ignored in the days before
Coleridge and especially before Thomas Carlyle. James Boswell, who could produce an assortment of intelligible phrases in that language, appears to have been an
exception. (17)

It does not take great critical imagination to argue that Lessing's ideas,
had they been within the reach of Blair, would have fallen on fertile ground. But
Blair never discovered what the great German aesthetician had formulated, and
his views on the interplay of the arts remained contradictory, thus forming one
of the few weak points in what otherwise appears as a collection of lucid and profound critical insights.

Dr. Johnson, likewise, would have been a receptive reader of Lessing's
thoughts, for in 1759 he wrote in his Rasselas a famous passage that is usually
quoted in support of the idea that the eighteenth century was interested in the general rather than the particular, but which in our context can be interpreted in the
sense of a warning against tedious description:

'The business of a poet,' said Imlac, 'is to examine,
not the individual, but the species; to remark
general properties and large appearances: he does
not number the streaks of the tulip, or describe the
different shades in the verdure of the forest. He
is to exhibit, in his portraits of nature, such prominent and striking features, as recall the original
to every mind; and must neglect the minuter discri-

minations, which one may have remarked, and another have
neglected, for those characteristics, which are alike
obvious to vigilance and carelessness. (18)

Boswell recorded Johnson's brief but poignant differentiation between painting and
poetry that occurred much later, during a conversation in 1784, the year of his
death:

When I observed to him that Painting was so far
inferiour to Poetry that the story or even emblem
which it communicates must be previously known, and
mentioned as a natural and laughable instance of
this that a little Miss on seeing a picture of
Justice with the scales had exclaimed to me, 'See,
there's a woman selling sweetmeats;' he said,
'Painting, Sir, can illustrate, but cannot inform.' (19)

But Johnson knew no German, although at one point he studied the Friesian language, and he, too, remained ignorant of Lessing's achievements.

The Laokoon, then, captured the attention of the English very late. From
1820 on references to the work appeared more and more frequently, but extended
critiques were not forthcoming until the second half of the nineteenth century. In
1853 E. C. Beasley published his translation, entitled Laocoon; An Essay on the
Limits of Painting and Poetry, with a critical introduction by T. Burbridge. Kenwood asserts that Thomas Babington Macauley read Ross's translation several
times and confessed in a footnote in the Life and Works of Goethe (1855) that the
Laokoon excited both his wonder and despair, because it appeared to him to be
totally beyond his own abilities. An extensive search, however, has failed so far
to prove that Macaulay ever wrote a life of Goethe, so that Kenwood's allegation
has to be accepted with a certain amount of caution. (20) In 1874 appeared Sir
Robert Phillimore's translation prefixed by a significant preface, in which Phillimore deals with the great importance of the work; and in 1907 Thomas G. Tucker
wrote words of supreme approbation: "... it [Laokoon] has perhaps influenced
more minds than any other work on aesthetics ever written except those of Aristotle and Longinus." (21)

Thus, Lessing's fame as an aesthetician at long last was established in
England. But in the eighteenth century he had been all but ignored, and although
major aestheticians adhered at times to precepts similar to Lessing's, they supported ut pictura poesis ideas just as often, so that it is difficult to avoid the impression that there prevailed a continuing state of confusion with regard to the
fundamental problem of whether the arts should be clearly distinguished.

2. LESSING AND HERDER

The situation was entirely different in Germany. The publication of Laokoon immediately caused great excitement and a flood of reviews, which in most cases were highly favorable. One impressive critic, however, stepped forward to discuss Lessing's achievement in a rather sceptical vein. This was Johann Gottfried Herder. Herder apparently had subscribed completely to Lessing's theoretical conclusions immediately after the publication of the work. In a letter to Johann Georg Scheffner, a close friend and literatus, dated October 4, 1766, he had written: "Ich finde es sehr billig, genau und fruchtbar, dass das Nebeneinander für den Mahler, und das Aufeinander für den Dichter ist." (22) But soon he began to have second thoughts on the subject, and by 1769, writing the "Erstes Wäldchen" of the four <u>Kritische Wälder</u>, he attacked the very foundation of Lessing's aesthetic concepts.

Herder at first overwhelms the reader with a mass of what he himself is pleased to call "critical rubbish" ("kritischer Schutt"), lengthy discussions whether the Homeric heroes really roared when wounded, and whether Lessing was justified in claiming that Sophocles's <u>Philoctetes</u> was centered on the violent expression of the hero's awful pain, questions which Herder answers in the negative. When he finally approaches the crux of the matter, he begins quite logically with an examination of Lessing's conception of the <u>punctum temporis</u>. Lessing, it will be remembered, held that in the selection of the "most pregnant moment" on the time-line of an action, a painter or sculptor has to avoid the representation of the very crisis, such as the roaring of Laocoon, because of the transitory nature of the crisis and the inability of the spectator's imagination to contemplate a meaningful progression of the action. (23) Now Herder denies the validity of this argument by pointing out that, in a sense, everything in this world is transitory:

> Jeder Zustand in der Welt ist so mehr oder minder
> transitorisch. Sulzer (24) hat sich mit gesenktem Haupte,
> mit einem vom Finger unterstützten Kinne, und mit
> tiefer Philosophischer Mine stechen lassen. Nach Hr.
> Lessings Grundsatze müsste man ihn im Bild anreden:
> Philosoph, wirst du bald deine Aesthetik ausgedacht
> haben? stirbt dir nicht dein gesenkter Kopf, und dein
> erhabner Finger? Seufzender Laokoon, wie lange wirst
> du seufzen? So oft ich dich sehe, ist dir noch die
> Brust beklemmt, der Unterleib eingezogen? ein transi-
> torischer Augenblick, ein Seufzer, ist bei dir wider-
> natürlich verlängert. Der Donnerwerfende Jupiter, und
> die schreitende Diana, der den Atlas tragende Herkules,
> und jede Figur in der mindsten Handlung und Bewegung,
> ja auch nur in jedem Zustande des Körpers ist alsdenn
> widernatürlich verlängert: denn keine derselben dauret
> ja ewig. So wird also, wenn die vorstehende Meinung
> Grundsatz würde, das Wesen der Kunst zerstört. (25)

It is obvious that in this paragraph Herder attempts to avoid the temporal element altogether as irrelevant in the distinction of the arts. His reasoning seems to suggest that, since the whole creation is irrevocably placed under the sway of time, it is futile to speak of "coexistent" as opposed to "successive" signs. If Herder had introduced his "work - energy" dichotomy on this basis, he would have had a reasonably firm foundation. But Herder did not possess the strictly logical mind of a Lessing. Thus, in his discussion of the differences between painting and poetry he essentially keeps Lessing's coexistence and succession, and merely rearranges the emphasis. The signs of painting are, indeed, "coexistent," the signs of poetry, however, are not so much distinguished by their succession as by their arbitrary nature. The coexistent character of its signs is the very essence of painting, the succession of the signs of poetry, on the other hand, is only an inevitable restriction, a "conditio sine qua non":

> Malerei wirkt ganz im Raume, neben einander, durch
> Zeichen, die die Sache natürlich zeigen. Poesie aber
> nicht so durch die Succession, wie jene durch den
> Raum. Auf der Folge ihrer artikulirten Töne beruhet
> das nicht, was in der Malerei auf dem Nebeneinanderseyn
> der Theile beruhete. Das Successive ihrer Zeichen ist
> nichts als conditio, sine qua non, und also blos einige
> Einschränkung: das Coexistiren der Zeichen in der
> Malerei aber ist Natur der Kunst, und der Grund der
> Malerischen Schönheit. Poesie, wenn sie freilich durch
> auf einander folgende Töne, das ist, Worte wirkt: so
> ist doch das Aufeinanderfolgen der Töne, die Succession
> der Worte nicht der Mittelpunkt ihrer Wirkung. (p. 135)

Herder, thus, applies a combination of the "coexistent - successive" and the "natural - artificial" dichotomies to differentiate between the two arts. He defends his method by comparing painting with music, an art that is based on both "successive" and "natural signs." In the case of such a comparison, he reasons, it is correct to say that the only difference between the two arts lies in the fact that one of them functions in space, the other in time. Words, however, are not in the same category with musical tones. They are mostly arbitrary and whatever natural aspects they may have, can be safely neglected. These speculations lead Herder to his "work - energy" distinction. The differences between painting and sculpture on one side, and poetry, music, and dance on the other, are based on the fact that the arts which function in space present completed "works," whereas the arts that exist in time are efficacious through the "energy" which they release at any given point:

> Malerei wirkt im Raume, und durch eine künstliche
> Vorstellung des Raums. Musik, und alle energischen
> Künste wirken nicht blos in, sondern auch durch die
> Zeitfolge, durch einen künstlichen Zeitwechsel der
> Töne. Liesse sich nicht das Wesen der Poesie auch
> auf einen solchen Hauptbegriff bringen, da sie durch
> willkührliche Zeichen, durch den Sinn der Worte auf die
> Seele wirkt? Wir wollen das Mittel dieser Wirkung

Kraft nennen: und so, wie in der Metaphysik Raum,
Zeit und Kraft drei Grundbegriffe sind, sie die Mathe-
matischen Wissenschaften sich alle auf eine dieser
Begriffe zurückführen lassen; so wollen wir auch in
der Theorie der schönen Wissenschaften und Künste
sagen: die Künste, die Werke liefern, wirken im
Raume; die Künste die durch Energie wirken, in der
Zeitfolge; die schönen Wissenschaften, oder vielmehr
die einzige schöne Wissenschaft, die Poesie, wirkt
durch Kraft -. Durch Kraft, die einmal den Worten
beiwohnt, durch Kraft, die zwar durch das Ohr geht,
aber unmittelbar auf die Seele wirket. Diese Kraft
ist das Wesen der Poesie, nicht aber das Coexistente,
oder die Succession. (p. 137)

Now, this paragraph is far from clear. Herder strives hard to distinguish
poetry not only from the arts which result in a complete work, but also from those
which are based on energy, but whose signs are "natural," rather than "artificial,"
such as music. He introduces a new term, "Kraft," that is "force," a force that
impresses the energy in poetry directly on the human soul. The reader can hardly
be blamed for desiring to know more about the exact nature of this force and the
differences between poetry and the other energetic arts that it entails, and he
would like to know, whether painting, particularly allegorical and historical painting, exerts a similar kind of force on the human mind. But Herder is not prepared
to accomodate his reader with the appropriate information. Having discovered
some flaws in Lessing's theory, he is more content with raising questions than
providing answers. It is certainly true that Lessing, as Herder is quick to point
out, failed to compare poetry with music, dance, and rhetoric in order to obtain
a complete theory of this art that could not be obtained by merely contrasting it
with painting (cf. p. 133), and it is equally true that he did not pay enough attention to the circular nature of many of Homer's images, in which the father of
poetry plays repeatedly on the same tones, the same aspects of a thought, so that
the similes contain an element of repetition, which, in a way, is static (cf. pp. 132 -
133). Herder, however, solves little. He rather offers ultimately only a somewhat
watered-down version of Lessing's ideas.
Thus, on the important topic of poetic description Herder in general argues
that Lessing was too narrow in radically restricting description. Static description
is quite legitimate, since succession is not the major criterion of poetry. He defends Ariosto's description of the fay Alcina by claiming that the poet was far from
representing the divine creature in her complete beauty to be experienced in its
totality. Rather, he was content with describing one beautiful part after the other,
so that her charms would be enjoyed step by step (cf. p. 162). This sounds
logical, but elsewhere Herder surprises with the declaration that he, too, delights
in action, passion, and feeling, and that he fully rejects mere static description,
especially if it takes up considerable space:

Handlung, Leidenschaft, Empfindung! - auch ich

> liebe sie in Gedichten über alles: auch ich hasse
> nichts so sehr, als todte stillstehende Schilder-
> ungssucht, insonderheit, wenn sie Seiten, Blätter,
> Gedichte einnimmt; aber nicht mit dem tödtlichen
> Hasse, um jedes einzelne ausführliche Gemälde, wenn
> es auch coexistent geschildert würde, zu verbannen,
> nicht mit dem tödtlichen Hasse, um jeden Körper nur
> mit einem Beiworte an der Handlung Theil nehmen zu
> lassen, und denn auch nicht aus dem nämlichen Grunde,
> weil die Poesie in successiven Tönen schildert, oder
> weil Homer dies und jenes macht, und nicht macht - -
> um deswillen nicht. (p. 157)

It is evident that Herder is trying to tone down the contradiction which this rather astonishing statement raises in the face of his own theory. He claims to be less absolute than Lessing, but the whole argument seems to be suspended in midair. If poetry is not characterized by succession, what then are Herder's reasons for preferring action and passion to lengthy description? One searches quite in vain for an answer. Is it to be found in the fact that poetry, as "energy," influences directly the imagination, that the ear serves only as an intermediary, and that memory plays no role? (26) Perhaps, but the reader cannot be certain.

In the final analysis Herder's method proves to be too loose, his style too rambling to provide an alternative theory to Lessing's Laokoon. He obviously was fully aware of the situation. The last sentence of the "Erstes Wäldchen" contains an apology for the nebulous character of the essay:

> In mehr als einer Sprache hat das Wort Wälder den
> Begriff von gesammelten Materien ohne Plan und
> Ordnung; ich wünschte nur, dass meine Leser die
> etwas trocknen und verschlossenen Pfade dieses
> ersten Theils überstehen möchten, um hinter denselben
> zu freiern Aussichten zu gelangen. (p. 188)

Notwithstanding the vague nature of the "Erstes Wäldchen," it is not only interesting because it raises fundamental questions regarding Lessing's theory, but also because it establishes a link to James Harris. Herder was the first German aesthetician to acknowledge the importance of Harris's Three Treatises. (27) Three pages of the essay are devoted to Harris, and Herder confesses to have been strongly influenced by this "profound English thinker" ("scharfsinniger Engländer"). Evidently the "energy - work" idea stemmed from the "First Treatise." Herder finds only one fault with Harris, namely that he placed too much emphasis on a silly competition of painting, music, and poetry, in order to establish a hierarchy of the arts. But on the whole he considers him preferable to Lessing and more advanced in his theories - with all due respect for Harris, certainly an unwarranted judgment.

3. CONCLUSION

Lessing's _Laokoon_ emerges in this study as the most thorough investigation of a problem that formed one of the basic issues of eighteenth century aesthetics. Short of representing a complete system dealing with all the differences and similarities of the arts, it is, nevertheless a work which in the words of André Gide "... it is good to reiterate or contradict every thirty years." (28)

It is safe to say that no critic, before or after Lessing, has succeeded in formulating the problems raised by the phrase _ut pictura poesis_ more clearly than the author of _Laokoon_. Lessing's great achievement was undoubtedly due to his considerable logical powers, but part of the credit should go to his predecessors in Germany, France, and especially England. The possible contributions of England have been the main topic of this thesis, and it has been found that unexpectedly rich sources of conjectures and ideas presented themselves to Lessing. To what degree he availed himself of this mine can hardly be answered precisely, but it seems reasonably evident that he did derive valuable suggestions from the pioneering work of a number of English theoreticians. Such aestheticians as Shaftesbury, Jacob, "Hermes Harris", Burke, and Kames have been discussed in detail in connection with their ideas concerning the validity of the "sister arts" concept, and it has been shown that some of their theories were already remarkably advanced, although they never quite reached Lessing's precision.

The definitive theory of the efficacy of the arts yet remains to be written. The questions raised by the _ut pictura poesis_ school and their lively opponents have not been fully answered. In recent years Lessing's thoughts have received increasing attention, and it is possible to distinguish three different camps of critics concerning the evaluation of his work. One group of critics under the leadership of Jean Hagstrum continue to adhere to an unmitigatedly egalitarian position, proclaiming the close similarity of the arts. A second school, represented particularly by the German critic Bruno Markwardt, would like to pursue the question on the basis of Herder's thoughts, arguing that the arts should be separated, but not on Lessing's grounds. A third party, finally, accepts Lessing at least conditionally.

Frank Joseph in _The Widening Gyre; Crisis and Mastery in Modern Literature_ (1963) goes furthest with his support of Lessing. Criticizing modern poetry in the light of Lessing's distinction of the different sensuous media that are used by the various arts, he points out that modern poets such as Ezra Pound and T. S. Eliot strive to achieve a spatial form of poetry by substituting a kind of coexistence of various disconnected thoughts and images for the traditional logical sequence of arguments, ideas, and feelings. This spatial form, contends Joseph, must ultimately fail, since the character of language is based on time, not space.

René Wellek agrees with Lessing that extended enumerations of static details are tedious:

> Lessing's main distinction between the arts of
> space and time, though debatable, is basically
> sound. His objections to static descriptions in

literature were not only salutory in their time,
but, if properly qualified, are applicable even
today: most of us skip the formal descriptions in
the novels of Scott or Balzac. Lessing is certainly
putting his finger on the issue when he points to
the difficulty of our forming a whole from an accumu-
lation of traits, and he is also right in opposing
the stress on visualization in literature, which in
the 18th century was favored by the current interpretation of the term "imagination" as practically
identical with visual imagination. Literature
does not evoke sensuous images, or if it does, does
so only incidentally, occasionally, and intermittently.
Even in the depiction of a fictional character the
writer need not suggest visual images at all. We
can scarcely visualize most of Dostoevsky's or Henry
James's characters, while we know their states of
mind, their motivations, evaluations, attitudes,
and desires very completely. Lessing stresses
characterization by the single trait, by the one
Homeric epithet, the method which is substantially
that of Tolstoy or Thomas Mann. (29)

Emil Staiger maintains in his <u>Grundbegriffe der Poetik</u> that Lessing was
concerned only with the boundaries of epic poetry, since lyrical poetry does not
describe at all and represents neither bodies nor actions. With this restriction in
mind Staiger essentially approves of Lessing's conclusions, although he suggests
that Lessing had perhaps too dramatic a conception of epic poetry:

Dennoch lässt sich nicht verkennen, dass Lessing an
die Dichtung allzusehr den dramatischen Masstab
anlegt, schon in der Abhandlung über die Fabel, wo
er sich alle Schilderungen, die mit der moralischen
Schlusspointe nichts zu schaffen haben, verbittet und
wenig Verständnis hat für die reizvollen epischen Züge
bei Lafontaine.
        Damit wird jedoch Lessings These höchstens
zurechtgerückt, nicht widerlegt. Der Widerstreit
zwischen Vorstellung und fortschreitender Rede bleibt
bestehen. Es fragt sich nur, ob der epische Dichter
ihn nicht auf eine Weise schlichte, welche der
Anschauung besser gerecht wird als die dramatische
Zielstrebigkeit. (30)

Staiger's thoughts attain their full meaning only, when one is aware of his
definition of the terms "lyrical," "epic," and "dramatic." Staiger does not refer
to literary genres, but rather to three different styles or tones of writing. Thus,

"lyrical" suggests a poetry that is nostalgic in nature, looks back to the past and emphasizes the syllable. "Epic" writing is enamoured with "being," embraces the world in complete harmony, exists wholly in the present, and emphasizes the word. "Dramatic," finally, is that poetry which bristles with suspense, looks constantly to the future, and is centered on the sentence. For Staiger the lyrical tone is too languid, while the dramatic style is torn and twisted, so that "epic" poetry emerges as the highest form of literary expression. Staiger would obviously like to avoid Lessing's strong emphasis of time in poetry, because this is too suggestive of the "dramatic" style, and he does find an ingenious compromise. Even the "epic" poet works in time, since language is temporal, but he can afford to linger with the moment, to proceed slowly and unhurriedly step by step, to confront the reader with each scene long enough to enable him to form an appropriate conception of the poet's imagination, but not so long that his memory is overtaxed:

> Als auf die Sprache angewiesener Dichter schreitet
> der Epiker fort und folgt dem Nacheinander der Zeit,
> im Gegensatz zu dem bildenden Künstler, der dasteht
> und das Nebeneinander und Hintereinander des Raumes
> erfasst. Bei jedem Schritt aber hält der Epiker inne
> und sieht sich von festem Standpunkt aus einen festen
> Gegenstand an. Jetzt dies, jetzt jenes: die Zeit
> vergeht, indem der Dichter ein Bild nach dem anderen
> wahrnimmt und dem Hörer zeigt. Er wird so lange
> verweilen, bis das Bild sich deutlich eingeprägt
> hat, aber nicht länger, als der Hörer im Nacheinander
> der Worte noch das Nebeneinander, das sie bedeuten,
> leicht im Gedächtnis behalten kann. Alles, was Lessing
> an der Kunst Homers rühmt, lässt sich so erklären,
> ohne dass man genötigt wäre, auch den Uebertreibungen
> zuzustimmen, zu denen ihn der polemische Eifer hinriss.
> (p. 112)

Allowing for its restricted scope this is probably the wisest statement that has been pronounced on the question of ut pictura poesis. The most poetic, however, was formulated at the very end of the eighteenth century by Friedrich Schlegel:

> Die Poesie ist Musik für das innere Ohr, und Malerei
> für das innere Auge; aber gedämpfte Musik, aber
> verschwebende Malerei. (31)

FOOTNOTES

CHAPTER I

1. (London, 1747).

2. See Tableaux tirés de l'Iliade, de l'Odyssée d'Homère et de l'Enéide de
   Virgile; avec des observations générales sur le costume (Paris, 1757).

3. William G. Howard deserves the credit for having introduced the topic in
   his essay on "Ut Pictura Poesis," PMLA, XXIV (1909), 40 - 123. Then
   followed Cicely Davies's "Ut Pictura Poesis," MLR, XXX (April, 1935),
   159 - 169; Rennselaer Lee's "Ut Pictura Poesis: The Humanistic Theory of
   Painting," Art Bulletin, XXII (December, 1940), 197 - 269; and Wladyslaw
   Folkierski's "Ut pictura poesis, ou l'étrange fortune du De arte graphica de
   Du Fresnoy en Angleterre," Revue de Littérature comparée, XXVII (October - December, 1953), 385 - 402. Jean Hagstrum devoted a widely acknowledged book to the topic entitled The Sister Arts; the Tradition of Literary
   Pictorialism and English Poetry from Dryden to Gray (Chicago, 1958).
   Rémy G. Saisselin examined the idea of "the sister arts" in eighteenth-century France in "Ut Pictura Poesis: DuBos to Diderot," JAAC, XX (Fall,
   1961), 145 - 156, Ralph Cohen investigated the problem in "Ut Pictura
   Poesis," a chapter in The Art of Discrimination (Berkeley and Los Angeles,
   1964), pp. 188 - 247, and Harvey D. Goldstein provokingly reversed
   Horace's phrase in "Ut Poesis Pictura: Reynolds on Imitation and Imagination," ECS, I, No. 3 (Spring, 1968), 213 - 235.

4. PMLA, XXII (1907), 608 - 632.

5. (Frankfurt a. M., 1937).

6. (Berlin, 1956).

7. (Berkeley and Los Angeles, 1964), pp. 131 - 187.

8. Hagstrum (Chicago, 1958), p. 155.

9. Hagstrum, p. 10; Simonides, a Greek lyric poet, lived from ca. 556 - 467
   B. C.

10. "Traditum est etiam Homerum caecum fuisse; at eius picturam, non poësin
    videmus."; in Ciceron, Tusculanes, société d'edition "Les Belles Lettres,"
    II, V, 114 (Paris, 1960), 160.

11. Horace, ed. E. C. Wickham, II (Oxford, 1903), ll 360 - 365.

12. Op. cit., pp. 59 - 61.

13. ed. critica a cura di Luigi Mallà (Florence, 1950). For a critical discus-
    sion in German see Rudolf von Eitelberger von Edelberg, Quellenschriften
    für Kunstgeschichte und Kunsttechnik des Mittelalters und der Renaissance ...,
    XI (Vienna, 1877), 89.

14. <u>Poetices</u> <u>Libri</u> <u>Septem</u>, editio quinta (Heidelberg, 1617), p. 401.

15. <u>Die</u> <u>Entstehung</u> <u>der</u> <u>neueren</u> <u>Aesthetik</u> (Stuttgart, 1886), p. 125.

16. <u>The</u> <u>Sister</u> <u>Arts</u>, p. 59.

17. <u>Politique</u> <u>Discourses</u> <u>on</u> <u>trueth</u> <u>and</u> <u>lying</u>. An <u>instruction</u> <u>to</u> <u>Princes</u> <u>to</u> <u>keepe</u> <u>their</u> <u>faith</u> <u>and</u> <u>promise</u>... <u>Translated</u> <u>out</u> <u>of</u> <u>French</u>... <u>by</u> <u>Sir</u> <u>E</u>. <u>Hoby</u> in <u>Elizabethan</u> <u>Critical</u> <u>Essays</u>, ed. G. Gregory Smith, I (Oxford, 1904), 342.

18. See <u>The</u> <u>Works</u> <u>of</u> <u>John</u> <u>Dryden</u>, ed. Sir Walter Scott, revised and corrected by George Saintsbury, XVII (London, 1892), 289 - 335.

19. <u>The</u> <u>Works</u> <u>of</u>... <u>Jonathan</u> <u>Richardson</u>, ed. Jonathan Richardson jun. (London, 1773), p. 263.

20. "Ut Pictura Poesis: DuBos to Diderot"; <u>JAAC</u>, XX (Fall, 1961) 146.

21. "Réflexions sur la peinture," <u>Vies</u> <u>d'artiste</u> <u>du</u> <u>XVIIIe</u> <u>Siècle</u>, ed. André Fontaine (Paris, 1910), p. 136.

22. Harris, p. 156.

23. "Treatise the First: Concerning Art, a Dialogue," <u>Three</u> <u>Treatises</u> (London, 1744), 38 - 41.

24. "English Neoclassical Criticism: An Outline Sketch," <u>Critics</u> <u>and</u> <u>Criticism</u> <u>Ancient</u> <u>and</u> <u>Modern</u>, by R. S. Crane and others, ed. R. S. Crane, (Chicago, 1952), pp. 372 - 388.

25. <u>The</u> <u>Sublime</u>; <u>A</u> <u>Study</u> <u>of</u> <u>Critical</u> <u>Theories</u> <u>in</u> <u>XVIII</u> - <u>England</u> (Ann Arbor, 1960), p. 1.

26. In <u>The</u> <u>Gleaner</u>, ed. Nathan Drake, I, v (London, 1811), 32.

27. <u>The</u> <u>Art</u> <u>of</u> <u>Discrimination</u>, p. 142.

28. "Descriptions in poetry, the reasons why they please," <u>Lay</u> <u>Monastery</u>, No. 39 (Feb. 12, 1713), in <u>The</u> <u>Gleaner</u>, ed. Nathan Drake, I, vii (London, 1811), 45.

29. <u>A</u> <u>New</u> <u>Introduction</u> <u>to</u> <u>the</u> <u>Classics</u> (London, 1718), p. 238.

30. <u>Lectures</u> <u>on</u> <u>Poetry</u>; <u>Read</u> <u>in</u> <u>the</u> <u>Schools</u> <u>of</u> <u>Natural</u> <u>Philosophy</u> (1713), transl. anon. from Latin (London, 1742), p. 17.

31. <u>The</u> <u>Works</u> <u>of</u> <u>Tobias</u> <u>Smollett</u>, ed. George Saintesbury, XI (London, n.d.), 94 - 95.

32. Locke, ed. Rev. R. H. Quick (Cambridge, 1899), p. 200.

33. Addison, ed. Donald F. Bond, III, cxi-cxxi (Oxford, 1965), 536 - 537.

34. Addison uses in these essays the terms "imagination" and "fancy" inter-changeably, or "promiscuously," as he calls it.

35. Already in 1771 Tobias Smollett had Matthew Bramble communicate to Dr. Lewis the pleasure he derived from the pictures of the "landscape painter T...": "If there is any taste for ingenuity left in a degenerate age, fast sinking into barbarism, this artist, I apprehend, will make a capital figure, as soon as his works are known." op. cit., p. 99.

36. Baumgarten coined the term "asthetica" already in 1734 in his dissertation with the title Meditationes philosophicae de nonnullis ad poema pertinentibus. The dissertation has been generally overlooked and most scholars continue to assert that the famous word appeared for the first time in 1750 in Baumgarten's collected opus Aesthetica.

37. Reflections on Poetry, transl. from Meditationes... by Karl Aschenbrenner and William Holther (Berkeley and Los Angeles, 1954).

38. Ibid., p. 52.

39. See A Philosophical Enquiry into the Origin of our Ideas of the Sublime and Beautiful (1757), ed. J. T. Boulton (London and New York, 1958), especially II, iv; V, i - vii.

40. Breitinger (Zurich, 1740), p. 14.

CHAPTER II

1. In Quellenschriften für Kunstgeschichte und Kunsttechnik des Mittelalters und der Renaissance, ed. Rudolf von Eitelberger von Edelberg, XV - XVII (Vienna, 1882).

2. "Ut Pictura Poesis," PMLA, XXIV (1909), 49 - 50; cf. Ludwig, XV, 20, 22, 38, 42, 48, 54, 64.

3. Howard, 50; cf. Ludwig, XV, 24, 30.

4. Howard, 48 - 49; cf. Ludwig, XV, 8, 16, 18, 20, 30, 32, 38, 40, 44, 46, 50.

5. Varchi (Florence, 1590), pp. 226 - 230.

6. Ibid., p. 229.

7. "A Treatise de Carmine Pastorali, "; trans.from Dissertatio de Carmine Pastorali in Eclogae Sacrae (1659) prefixed to Thomas Creech's translation Idylliums of Theocritus (London, 1684), Augustan Reprint Society (Ann Arbor, 1947), p. 65. Rapin continues: "He [Virgil] doth it in five verses, Theocritus runs out into thirty, which certainly is an argument of a wit that is very much at leisure, and unable to moderate his force."

8. "Of Descriptions"; Epick Poem (trans. from Traité du poème epique, 1675), trans. W. J. (London, 1695), p. 242.

9. Anecdotes, Observations, and Characters, of Books and Men (1820), ed. Samuel W. Singer (London, 1858), pp. 139 - 140.

10. "Prologue to the Satires"; The Works of Alexander Pope, ed. William Warburton, II (London, 1788), 185, 11. 147 - 150.

11. Editorial footnote to "The First Epistle of the Second Book of Horace"; The Works of Alexander Pope, ed. William Warburton, II (London, 1788), 279.

12. Cohen, p. 143.

13. The Dublin Journal (March 12, 1726), in Hibernicus' Letters, I (London, 1729), 424 - 425.

14. In Miscellanea Aurea: or the Golden Medley (London, 1720), pp. 22 - 23.

15. ed. J. T. Boulton, (London, New York, 1958), p. 167.

16. In Anfangsgründe aller schönen Wissenschaften, II (Halle/Saale, 1749), 615, Meier defined the word as follows: "Die Bezeichnungskunst (characteristica) ist die Wissenschaft der Zeichen, sie enthält also die Regeln, das Bezeichnungsvermögen zu verbessern, und dasselbe gehörig zu gebrauchen."

17. Poetics, trans. W. H. Fyfe (London, 1953), pp. 5 - 6.

18. op. cit., pp. 307 - 308.

19. Shaftesbury, fifth ed., III (London, 1732), 353.

20. See Poesie und Nichtpoesie.

21. Shaftesbury, p. 387.

22. Dubos., seventh ed., I (Paris, 1770), 413 - 414.

23. Werke, ed. B. Suphan, III (Berlin, 1879).

24. See Ludwig Goldstein, "Moses Mendelssohn und die deutsche Aesthetik," Teutonia, III (Königsberg, 1904).

25. In an "Advertisement to the Reader," prefixed to the Three Treatises, Harris declares that: "One of his reasons for adding notes was, to give weight to his assertions from the authority of antient writers. But his chief and principal reason was, to excite (if possible) the curiosity of readers, to examine with stricter attention those valuable remains of antient literature."

26. Harris, p. 58n.

27. Ibid., p. 71.

28. See James Harris and the Influence of His Aesthetic Theories in Germany, unpubl. diss. University of Michigan. (Ann Arbor, 1929), p. 140.

29. Dubos's Réflexions was translated into English by Thomas Nugent under the title of Critical Reflections on Poetry, Painting, and Music, but not before 1748, four years after the first edition of the Three Treatises. Harris, however, did not have to resort to a translation.

30. In Moses Mendelssohns Schriften zur Metaphysik und Ethik sowie zur Religionsphilosophie, ed. Moritz Brasch (Leipzig, 1880), hereafter cited as Brasch.

31. Mendelssohn, p. 151: "Die Schönheit der äusserlichen Formen überhaupt ist nur ein sehr geringer Theil von ihren [der Natur] Absichten, und sie hat dieselben zuweilen grössern Absichten nachsetzen müssen."

32. Hildebrand Jacob, 1693 - 1739, only son of Colonel Sir John Jacob, third baronet of Bromley, Kent. He died in his father's lifetime. Besides The Curious Maid he wrote The Fatal Constancy, a tragedy (1723), which was acted five times at Drury Lane. Another work, The Nest of Plays (1738), consisting of three comedies which were played on the same night at Drury Lane, was emphatically damned. Beside Of the Sister Arts; an Essay (1734), which is given detailed attention in this thesis, he wrote another remarkable thesis entitled How the Mind Is Rais'd to the Sublime (1735).

33. Only Ralph Cohen mentions this work briefly, but in a different context. See The Art of Discrimination, pp. 43, 189, 212.

34. "Pro A. Licinio archia poeta oratio"; Cicéron, Discours, société d'edition "Les Belles Lettres," XII, i (Paris, 1957), 35.

35. Jacob (London, 1734), p. 3.

36. Harris, p. 85.

37. Brasch, p. 167.

38. Kames, I (London, 1763), 121 - 122.

39. See Lessing, "Beschluss des Dreihundertzweiundreissigsten Briefes, 4. Julii 1765"; in "Briefe die neueste Literatur betreffend"; Gesammelte Werke, ed. Paul Rilla, IV (Berlin, 1955), 436 - 437, hereafter cited as Rilla.

40. "Der Ursprung unserer Ideen vom Erhabenen und Schönen"; in "Bibliothek der schönen Wissenschaften" (1758), Brasch, pp. 209 - 210.

CHAPTER III

1. "Das allgemeine vorzügliche Kennzeichen der griechischen Meisterstücke ist endlich eine edle Einfalt, und eine stille Grösse, sowohl in der Stellung als im Ausdruck. So wie die Tiefe des Meers allezeit ruhig bleibt, die Oberfläche mag noch so wüten, ebenso zeiget der Ausdruck in den Figuren der Griechen bei allen Leidenschaften eine grosse und gesetzte Seele." Gedanken, ed. Léon Mis, in Collections bilingue des classiques étrangers (Paris, n.d.), p. 142.

2. The protagonist of Sophocles's tragedy by the same name, written in 409 B.C., the only play by Sophocles that can be dated accurately.

3. As quoted by Lessing in Rilla, V, 13; see Winckelmann, pp. 142 - 144.

4. <u>Rilla</u>, V, 28.

5. It is quite conceivable that Lessing's ideas of the <u>punctum temporis</u> were inspired by Shaftesbury's intricate thoughts on the subject. Shaftesbury suggested the choice of the most suitable moment of an action to be depicted by the painter. But this was as far as he was prepared to go. Shaftesbury never renounced the validity of <u>ut pictura poesis</u>. He rather chose to re-affirm this principle by pointing out comparable restrictions imposed on the poet (see Chapter II).

6. <u>Rilla</u>, V, 77.

7. See <u>Tableaux tirés de l'Iliade, de l'Odyssée d'Homère et de L'Enéide de Virgile</u>; ... .

8. See Chapter II.

9. See <u>Rilla</u>, V, 117.

10. See Chapter II.

11. Considering Lessing's own predilection for didacticism as exemplified in his drama <u>Nathan der Weise</u> it may amuse the reader to discover his low view of didactic poetry: "..., denn da wo er [der dogmatische Dichter] dog-matisieret ist er kein Dichter. " (p. 127).

12. ll. 16 - 18; Lessing supplies his own translation in the text: "Wenn der poetische Stümper, sagt Horaz, nicht weiter kann, so fängt er an, einen Hain, einen Altar, einen durch anmutige Fluren sich schlängelnden Bach, einen rauschenden Strom, einen Regenbogen zu malen. " (p. 128).

13. <u>Prologue to the Satires</u>, ll. 341 - 342; 148 - 149; as quoted by Lessing, p. 129n.

14. Lessing, p. 129n; see editorial footnote to <u>The Works of Alexander Pope, in Verse and Prose, Containing the Principal Notes of Drs. Warburton and Warton</u>, ed. William Lisle Bowles, IV (London, 1806), 26.

15. See Section 4 of this Chapter.

16. <u>Rilla</u>, V, 308.

17. Dessoir (Berlin, 1902, reprinted Amsterdam, 1964), p. 116.

18. Sommer (Würzburg, 1892), p. VI.

19. <u>Kants Kritik der Urteilskraft; Ihre Geschichte und Systematik</u>, I (Halle/Saale, 1923), 149.

20. See <u>Rilla</u>, VII, 273 - 279.

21. See <u>Lessings Briefwechsel mit Mendelssohn und Nicolai</u>, ed. Robert Petsch (Leipzig, 1910).

22. In a letter to George August von Breitenbauch, a farmer and man of letters, dated December 12, 1755, Lessing mischievously quoted two English lines,

for which the recipient, who did not know English, needed a translator. Lessing indulged in this charming little joke to revenge himself for a number of illegible and incoherent passages in von Breitenbauch's preceeding favor. As potential translator of the two lines he recommended Mendelssohn or Müchler:

> Ich zitiere Ihnen deswegen eine englische Stelle, die Sie nicht verstehen, um mich wegen der unverständlichen Stellen, die in Ihrem Brief sind, zu rächen. Eine Sprache, die man nicht versteht, und eine Hand, die man nicht entziffern kann, gehen in Ansehung der Deutlichkeit in einem Paare. Sie können doch noch den H. Moses oder den H. Müchler um die Verdolmetschung bitten, mir aber kann den ähnlichen Dienst hier niemand erzeigen, auch nicht einmal mein Setzer in der Druckerei." Rilla, IX, 62.

And in a letter to Mendelssohn, dated April 28, 1756, he asked his friend to convey his greetings to Messrs. Naumann, Müchler, et al.; see Ibid., 69.

23. See Chapter II.

24. Hildebrand, p. 5.

25. Iliad, I, ll. 44 - 53; see Caylus, Tableaux, p. 7.

26. Rilla, V, 108.

27. Iliad, III, ll. 205 - 208, trans. Alexander Pope; as quoted by Burke in the Enquiry, p. 171.

28. Burke, p. 172.

29. Rilla, V, 157.

30. "... que vous me délivriez de ces raisonneurs importuns." Oeuvres complètes de Diderot, ed. J. Assézat, I (Paris, 1875), 386.

31. See Chapter I.

32. Meier basically distinguished between signum naturale, signum arbitrarium or artificiale, signa ninemonica, or rememorativa, signa demonstrativa, and signa prognostica. See Anfangsgründe, II, 609 - 610.

33. Gründliche Untersuchung von dem wahren Begriffe der Dichtkunst (Danzig, 1744), p. 114; as quoted in Bruno Markwardt, Geschichte der deutschen Poetik, II (Berlin, 1956), 30.

34. Beattie, Essays (London, 1762), pp. 146 - 147.

35. Fechner, "Lessings Laokoon und das Prinzip der bildenden Künste," Zeitschrift für bildende Kunst, XIX (Leipzig, 1884), 255.

36. See August Schmarsow, Erläuterungen und Kommentar zu Lessings Laokoon (Leipzig, 1909), p. 48.

37. Rilla, V, 262.

38. See Ibid., 307.

39. Ibid., 307 - 308.

40. Margaret Bieber, Laocoon: the Influence of the Group since Its Rediscovery (New York, 1942), p. 14.

41. See Rilla, IX, 318.

42. Ibid., 319 - 320.

43. Meier, II, 635.

44. See Rilla, III, 734.

45. See Ibid., 732.

46. See Rilla, V, 227.

47. Ibid., 262.

48. See Ibid., 149 - 154.

49. Ibid., 154.

50. Ibid., 327.

51. Epicurus, 341 - 370 B.C., was notable for his exposition of the atomistic theory of physics.

52. "Incognita"; Shorter Novels; Seventeenth Century, Everyman's Library, ed. Philip Henderson (London, New York, 1962), 263 - 264.

53. "The Adventures of Count Fathom"; The Works of Tobias Smollett, ed. George Saintsbury, XIII (London, n.d.), 3.

54. "Roderick Random"; The Works of Tobias Smollett, ed. George Saintsbury, III, 8.

55. The History of Tom Jones, a Foundling, ed. George Sherburn (New York, 1950), p. 544.

56. The Mysteries of Udolpho (1794), Everyman's Library, II (New York, 1962), 47.

57. (Boston, 1966), p. XI.

58. The World of Hogarth, p. 5.

59. "Epistle III; Of the Use of Riches," 11. 20 - 21; as quoted in a translators's footnote in The World of Hogarth, p. 10.

60. "On the Genius and Character of Hogarth"; The Works in Prose and Verse of Charles and Mary Lamb, ed. Thomas Hutchinson, I (London, 1908), 92.

61. See John M. Clapp, "An Eighteenth - Century Attempt at a Critical View of the Novel: The Bibliothèque Universelle des Romans," PMLA, New Series, XVIII (1910), 71.

62. <u>Rilla</u>, V, 323.

CHAPTER IV

1. His first work to be rendered into English was the <u>Fables</u> (<u>Fabeln</u>), a critical treatise written in 1759 and translated by John Richardson of Eworth in 1773. His plays followed a little later. <u>Minna von Barnhelm oder das Soldatenglück</u> (1767) was published under the title of <u>The Disbanded Officer, or the Baroness of Bruchsal</u> in London in 1786. It was staged on July 24 of that year at the Haymarket Theatre and ran nine nights. <u>Miss Sara Sampson</u> (1755) even caused transatlantic interest and was rendered into English by an anonymous "Citizen of Philadelphia" as <u>Lucy Sampson, or the Unhappy Heiress</u> in 1789. <u>Nathan der Weise</u> (1779) was translated by R. E. Raspe as <u>Nathan the Wise</u> only two years after its original publication, namely in 1781.

2. "Lessing in England, " <u>MLR</u>, IX (July, 1914), 346.

3. "Mr. Lessing is well known in the republic of letters, by several works, and particularly by his very ingenious Fables. - The performance now before us does honour to his taste and judgment, and will afford both entertainment and instruction to every Reader who is conversant with the fine arts. - It contains some observations, which appear to us to be very pertinent and judicious, upon Mr. Spence's <u>Polymetics,</u> Count Caylus's book entitled, <u>Tableaux tirés de l'Iliade de Homère</u>, etc., and Winckelmann's treatise of <u>Art among the Ancients. The Monthly</u> Review; or <u>Literary Journal: By Several Hands</u>, XXXVI (London, 1767), 575.

4. See Kenwood, p. 350.

5. See Chapter II.

6. Twenty-seven of these paintings depict various scenes of <u>Paradise Lost,</u> while <u>Paradise Regained</u> is represented by one. The most prominent compositions are: "Satan starting from the touch of Ithuriel's spear"; "Satan calling up his Legions"; "the Lubbar fiend"; "the Vision of the Deluge"; "Eve newly created, led to Adam"; and "Sin pursued by Death."

7. "See Lessing's <u>Laokoon</u>, Berlin, 1766. 8vo, " <u>Lectures on Painting, by the Royal Academicians. Barry, Opie, and Fuseli</u>, ed. Ralph N. Wornum (London, 1848), p. 407n.

8. <u>Lectures</u>, p. 407.

9. Seven of the ten episodes are at Hampton Court.

10. Wornum in "Introduction, " <u>Lectures on Painting, by the Royal Academicians,</u> etc., p. 53.

11. See Chapter II.

12. "Discourses"; <u>The Literary Works of Sir Joshua Reynolds</u>, ed. Henry William Beechy, I (London, 1878), 341 - 342.

13. Blair, ed. William Milner (Halifax, 1842), p. 60.

14. As quoted by Blair from "Summer," ll. 1042 - 1050, _Ibid._, p. 550.

15. See _Ibid._, pp. 537 - 542.

16. Salomon Gessner (1730 - 1788), a native of Zurich, was one of the most successful representatives of the literary rococo movement. His collection of pastorals, entitled _Idyllen_ (1756 - 1788), was translated into twenty languages. He also wrote a widely acknowledged epic, _Der Tod Abels_, in 1758.

17. On his Grand Tour Boswell visited Gottsched and Gellert in Berlin in October 1764, the only two German men of letters of any reputation that were available to him, since Lessing was in Breslau and Klopstock in Copenhagen.

18. _Rasselas_, ed. John Booth (London, 1817), p. 46.

19. _Boswell's Life of Johnson_, ed. George Birkbeck Hill, IV (Oxford, 1934), 321.

20. See "Lessing in England," p. 346. Kenwood refers to a footnote on p. 56 of Macauley's mysterious work.

21. _The Foreign Debt of English Literature_ (London, 1907), p. 240.

22. _Herders Sämmtliche Werke_, ed. Bernhard Suphan, III (Berlin, 1878), Xn, hereafter cited as _Suphan_.

23. See Chapter III.

24. Johann Georg Sulzer (1720 - 1779), aesthetician and professor of mathematics at the "Joachimsthalschen Gymnasium" in Berlin.

25. _Suphan_, III, 78.

26. "Ich lerne von Homer, dass die Wirkung der Poesie nie aufs Ohr, durch Töne, nicht aufs Gedächtnis, wie lange ich einen Zug aus der Succession behalte, sondern auf meine Phantasie wirke; von hieraus also, sonst nirgendsher, berechnet werden müsse." _Ibid._, 157.

27. Herder translates the title of Harris's work with a slight lack of precision as _Gespräche über die Kunst: über die Musik, Malerei und Poesie: über die Glückseligkeit_. He ignores that the second treatise is not written in the form of a dialogue.

28. "Le _Laocoon_ de Lessing est oeuvre qu'il est bon tous les trente ans de redire ou de contredire." _Prétextes_ (Paris, 1963; original ed. 1903), p. 25.

29. _A History of Modern Criticism: 1750 - 1950_, I (New Haven, 1955), 163.

30. Staiger (Zurich, 1951), p. 107.

31. _Athenäum_, I (Berlin, 1798), 45.

BIBLIOGRAPHY

Abram, Meyer H. The Mirror and the Lamp. New York, 1953.

Addison, Joseph. The Spectator, ed. Donald F. Bond. 5 vols. Oxford, 1965.

Alberti, Leon Battista. Della Pittura (1436), ed. critica a cura di Luigi Mallà, Florence, 1950.

Arbuckle James, untitled essay on description in The Dublin Journal, No. 50, March 12, 1726, in Hibernicus's Letters, I. London, 1729, 424 - 436.

Aristotle. Poetics, transl. W. H. Fyfe. London, 1953.

Babbitt, Irving. The New Laocoon, Boston, 1910.

Baeumler, Alfred. Kants Kritik der Urteilskraft; Ihre Geschichte und Systematik. 2 vols. Halle/Saale, 1923.

Baumgarten, Alexander Gottlieb. Aesthetica, facsimile of the 1750 - 1758 edition. Hildesheim, 1961.

—————————————. Reflections on Poetry, transl. from Meditationes philosophicae de nonnullis ad poema pertinentibus by Karl Aschenbrenner and William Holther. Berkeley and Los Angeles, 1954.

Beattie, James. Essays. London, 1762.

Bieber, Margaret. Laocoon; the Influence of the Group since Its Rediscovery, New York, 1942.

Blackmore, Sir Richard. "Parallel between Poetry and Painting" (1713), The Gleaner, ed. Nathan Drake. I, v - vi, London, 1811, 30 - 44.

Blackwall, Anthony. A New Introduction to the Classics, London, 1718.

Blair, Hugh. Lectures on Rhetoric and Belles Lettres, ed. William Milner. Halifax, 1842.

Bodmer, Johann Jacob. Johann Jacob Bodmers Critische Betrachtungen über die Poetischen Gemählde der Dichter, Zurich, 1741.

Borinski, Karl. Die Antike in Poetik und Kunsttheorie von Ausgang des klassischen Altertums bis auf Goethe und Wilhelm von Humboldt. 2 vols. Leipzig, 1914.

Le Bossu, René. Epick Poem, transl. from Traité du poème epique (1675) by W. J. London, 1695.

Boswell, James. Boswell's Life of Johnson, ed. George Birbeck Hill. 6 vols. Oxford, 1934.

Brämer, C. F. Gründliche Untersuchung von dem wahren Begriffe der Dichtkunst, Danzig, 1744.

Braitmaier, Friedrich. Geschichte der Poetischen Theorie und Kritik von den Diskursen der Maler bis auf Lessing, Frauenfeld, 1889.

Breitinger, Johann Jacob. Johann Jacob Breitingers Critische Dichtkunst Worinnen die Poetische Mahlerey in Absicht auf die Erfindung Im Grunde untersuchet und mit Beyspielen aus den berühmtesten Alten und Neuern erläutert wird, Zurich, 1740.

Burke, Edmund. A Philosophical Enquiry into the Origin of our Ideas of the Sublime and Beautiful (1757), ed. J. T. Boulton. London, New York, 1958.

Cassirer, Ernst. Die Philosophie der Aufklärung, Tübingen, 1932.

Cicero, Marcus Tullius. Ciceron, Tusculanes, société d'edition "Les Belles Lettres." 2 vols. Paris, 1960.

Clapp, John M. "An Eighteenth-Century Attempt at a Critical View of the Novel: The Bibliothèque Universelles des Romans," PMLA, New Series, XVIII (1910), 60 - 96.

Clutton - Brock, A. "Description in Poetry," Essays and Studies, Oxford, 1911, pp. 91 - 103.

Cohen, Ralph. The Art of Discrimination, Berkeley and Los Angeles, 1964.

Congreve, William. "Incognita" (1690), Shorter Novels; Seventeenth Century, Everyman's Library, London, New York, 1962.

Cooper, Anthony Ashley, Third Earl of Shaftesbury, "A Notion of the Tablature or Judgment of Hercules," Characteristics of Men, Manners, Opinions, Times, fifth ed., III, London, 1732, 345 - 391.

Crane, Ronald Salmon. "English Neoclassical Criticism: An Outline Sketch," Critics and Criticism: Ancient and Modern, by R. S. Crane and others, ed. R. S. Crane, Chicago 1952, pp. 372 - 388.

Daniello, Bernardino. La Poetica, Venice, 1536.

Davies, Cicely. "Ut Pictura Poesis," MLR, XXX (April, 1935), 159 - 169.

Dessoir, Max. Geschichte der neueren deutschen Psychologie (Berlin, 1902), reprinted Amsterdam, 1964.

Diderot, Denis. "Lettre sur les sourds et muets," Oeuvres complètes de Diderot, ed. J. Assézat, I, Paris, 1875, 343 - 428.

Dryden, John. The Works of John Dryden, ed. Sir Walter Scott, revised and corrected by George Saintsbury. 18 vols. London, 1882 - 1893.

Dubos, Jean Baptiste (Abbé). Réflexions critiques sur la poesie et sur la peinture (1719), seventh ed. 3 vols. Paris, 1770.

Fechner, H. "Lessings Laokoon und das Prinzip der bildenden Künste," Zeitschrift für bildende Kunst, XIX, Leipzig, 1884.

Fielding, Henry. The History of Tom Jones, a Foundling, ed. George Sherburn. New York, 1950.

Folkierski, Wladyslaw. "Ut pictura poesis, ou l'étrange fortune du De arte graphica de Du Fresnoy en Angleterre," Revue de Littérature comparée, XXVII (October - December, 1953), 385 - 402.

Frank, Joseph. The Widening Gyre; Crisis and Mastery in Modern Literature, New Brunswick, New Jersey, 1963.

Fuseli, Henry. Lectures on Painting, by the Royal Academicians. Barry, Opie, and Fuseli, ed. Ralph N. Wornum. London, 1848.

Ganz, Paul. Die Zeichnungen Hans Heinrich Füsslis, Olten, 1947.

Gide, André. Prétextes (1903), Paris, 1963.

Gilbert, Katharine and Kuhn, Helmut. A History of Esthetics (1939) Bloomington, Indiana, 1953.

Goldstein, Harvey D. "Ut Poesis Pictura: Reynolds on Imitation and Imagination," ECS, I, No. 3 (Spring, 1968), 213 - 235.

Goldstein, Ludwig. "Moses Mendelssohn und die deutsche Aesthetik," Teutonis, III, Königsberg, 1904.

Hagstrum, Jean. The Sister Arts; the Tradition of Literary Pictorialism and English Poetry from Dryden to Gray, Chicago, 1958.

Harris, James. Three Treatises, London, 1744.

Herder, Johann Gottfried. Herders Sämmtliche Werke, ed. Bernhard Suphan. 33 vols. Berlin, 1878.

Hildebrand, Jacob. Of the Sister Arts: an Essay, London, 1734.

Hoby, Edward Sir. Politique Discourses on trueth and lying. An instruction to Princes to keepe their faith and promise... Translated out of French... by Sir E. Hoby in Elizabethan Critical Essays, ed. G. Gregory Smith, I, Oxford, 1904.

Home, Henry, Lord Kames. Elements of Criticism (1762) second ed. Edinburgh, 1763.

Hoor, George J. ten. James Harris and the Influence of His Aesthetic Theories in Germany, unpubl. diss. University of Michigan, Ann Arbor, 1929.

Horatius, Quintus Flaccus. Horace, ed. E. C. Wickham. 2 vols. Oxford, 1903.

Howard, William G. "Burke among the Forerunners of Lessing," PMLA, XXII (1907), 608 - 632.

Howard, William G. "Ut Pictura Poesis," PMLA, XXIV (1909), 40 - 123.

Hughes, John. "Descriptions in poetry, the reasons why they please" (1713), The Gleaner, ed. Nathan Drake, I, vii, London, 1811, 45 - 54.

Johnson, Samuel. Rasselas, ed. John Booth. London, 1817.

Kenwood, Sydney H. "Lessing in England," MLR, IX, pt. 1 (April, 1914), 197 - 212; pt. 2 (July, 1914), 344 - 358.

Krieger, Murray. The Play and Place of Criticism, Baltimore, 1966.

Lamb, Charles. The Works in Prose and Verse of Charles and Mary Lamb, ed. Thomas Hutchinson. 2 vols. London, New York, Toronto, and Melbourne, 1908.

Lange, Karl. "Die ästhetische Illusion im 18. Jahrhundert," Zeitschrift für Aesthetik und allgemeine Kunstwissenschaft, I (1906), 30 - 43.

Leander, Folke. Lessing als ästhetischer Denker, Göteborg, 1942.

Lee, Rennselaer. "Ut Pictura Poesis: The Humanistic Theory of Painting," Art Bulletin, XXII (December, 1940), 197 - 269.

Lessing, Gotthold Ephraim. Gesammelte Werke, ed. Paul Rilla. 10 vols. Berlin, 1955.

_____. Lessings Briefwechsel mit Mendelssohn und Nicholai, ed. Robert Petsch. Leipzig, 1910.

Lichtenberg, Georg Christoph. The World of Hogarth: Lichtenberg's Commentaries on Hogarth's Engravings, transl. and ed. Ines and Gustav Herdan. Boston, 1966.

Lipking, Lawrence I. The Ordering of the Arts: Modes of Systematic Discourse in Eighteenth - Century English Histories and Criticism of Painting, Music, and Poetry, unpubl. diss. Cornell University, 1962.

Locke, Joh. Thoughts on Education (1693), ed. Rev. R. H. Quick. Cambridge, 1899.

Lomazzo, Giovanni Paolo. Trattato dell'arte de la Pittura... diviso in sette libri... Milan, 1584; transl. Richard Haydocke, Oxford, 1598.

Lotze Hermann. Geschichte der Aesthetik in Deutschland, Munich, 1868.

Manwaring, Elizabeth W. Italian Landscape in Eighteenth Century England, New York, 1925.

Markwardt, Bruno. Geschichte der deutschen Poetik, 4 vols. Berlin, 1956.

Marsh, Robert. "Harris and the Dialectic of Books," Four Dialectical Theories of Poetry, Chicago and London, 1965, pp. 129 - 170.

McGuinness, Arthur E. Henry Home, Lord Kames, New York: Twayne Publishers, 1970.

Meier, Georg Friedrich. Anfangsgründe aller schönen Wissenschaften, 3 vols. Halle/Saale, 1748 - 1750.

Mendelssohn, Moses. Moses Mendelssohns Schriften zur Metaphysik und Ethik sowie zur Religionsphilosophie, ed. Moritz Brasch. Leipzig, 1880.

Monk, Samuel H. The Sublime; A Study of Critical Theories in XVIII - England, Ann Arbor, 1960.

Nolte, Fred O. Lessing's Laokoon, Lancaster, Pa., 1940.

Oehlke, Waldemar. Lessing und seine Zeit, 2 vols. München, 1919.

Paulson, Ronald. Hogarth's Graphic Works, 2 vols. New Haven, 1965.

Pope, Alexander. The Works of Alexander Pope, ed. William Warburton. 6 vols. London, 1788.

_____. The Works of Alexander Pope, in Verse and Prose, Containing the Principal Notes of Drs. Warburton and Warton, ed. William Lisle Bowles. 10 vols. London, 1806.

Radcliffe, Anne. The Mysteries of Udolpho (1794), Everyman's Library, 2 vols. New York, 1962.

Rapin, René. "A Treatise de Carmine Pastorali," transl. from Dissertatio de Carmine Pastorali in Eclogae Sacrae (1659); prefixed to Thomas Creech's translation Idylliums of Theocritus (London, 1684), Augustan Reprint Society. Ann Arbor, 1947.

Reynolds, Joshua, Sir. The Literary Works of Sir Joshua Reynolds, ed. Henry William Beechey. 2 vols. London, 1878.

Richardson, Jonathan. The Works of ... Jonathan Richardson (1715), ed. Jonathan Richardson jun. London, 1773.

Rudowski, Victor Anthony. "Action as the Essence of Poetry: A Revaluation of Lessing's Argument," PMLA, LXXXII, No. 5 (October, 1967), 333 - 341.

Saintsbury, George. History of Criticism and Literary Taste in Europe, 3 vols. London, 1900.

S aisselin, Rémy G. "Ut Pictura Poesis: DuBos to Diderot," JAAC, XX (Fall, 1961), 145 - 156.

Scaliger, Julius Caesar. Poetices Libri Septem (1561), editio quinta. Heidelberg, 1617.

Schasler, Max. Kritische Geschichte der Aesthetik, Berlin, 1872.

Schlegel, Friedrich, and August Wilhelm. Athenäum, facsimile of 1798 - 1800 ed. Stuttgart, 1960.

Schmarsow, August. Erläuterungen und Kommentar zu Lessings Laokoon, Leipzig, 1909.

Smollett, Tobias. The Works of Tobias Smollett, ed. George Saintsbury. 12 vols. London, n. d.

Sommer, Robert. Grundzüge einer Geschichte der deutschen Psychologie und Aesthetik von Wolff - Baumgarten bis Kant - Schiller, Würzburg, 1892.

Spence, Joseph. Anecdotes, Observations, and Characters of Books and Men
(1820), ed. Samuel W. Singer, London, 1858.
_____. Polymetis: or, An Enquiry concerning the Agreement between
the Works of the Roman Poets, and the Remains of the Antient Artists,
London, 1747.

Staiger, Emil. Grundbegriffe der Poetik, Zurich, 1951.

Stein, Carl Heinrich von. Die Entstehung der neueren Aesthetik, Stuttgart, 1886.

Thorpe, Clarence. The Aesthetic Theory of Thomas Hobbes, with Special Reference
to His Contribution to the Psychological Approach in English Literary
Criticism, New York, 1965.

Trapp, Joseph. Lectures on Poetry; Read in the Schools of Natural Philosophy
(1713), transl. anon. from Latin. London, 1742.

Trevelyan, George Macauley. Illustrated English Social History, 4 vols. London,
1949 - 1952.

Trissino, Giovanni Giorgio. La Poetica, Vicenza, 1529.

Tubière, Anne-Claude-Philippe de, Comte de Caylus. "Réflections sur la peinture,"
Vies d'artiste du XVIIIe Siècle, ed. André Fontaine. Paris, 1910.
_____. Tableux Tirés de l'Iliade,
de l'Odyssée d'Homère et de l'Enéide de Virgile; avec des observations
générales sur le costume, Paris, 1757.

Tucker, Thomas George. The Foreign Debt of English Literature, London, 1907.

Twining, Thomas. Aristotle's Treatise on Poetry with Notes and Two Disserta-
tions on Poetical, and Musical Imitation (1789), 2 vols. London, 1812.

Vail, Curtis C. D. Lessing's Relation to the English Language and Literature in
Columbia University Germanic Studies, New Series, No. 3, New York,
1936.

Varchi, Benedetto. Lezzioni ... sopra diverse materie, poetiche e filosofiche,
Florence, 1590.

Vinci, Leonardo da. Trattato della Pittura in Quellenschriften für Kunstgeschichte
und Kunsttechnik des Mittelalters und der Renaissance, ed. Rudolf von
Eitelberger von Edelberg, XV - XVII, Vienna, 1882.

Walzel, Oskar. Poesie und Nichtpoesie, Frankfurt a. M. , 1937.

Warton, Joseph. An Essay on the Writings and Genius of Pope, London, 1756.

Webb, Daniel. An Inquiry into the Beauties of Painting, London, 1760.
_____. Remarks on the Beauties of Poetry, London, 1762.

Wellek, René. A History of Modern Criticism: 1750 - 1950, 4 vols. New Haven:
Yale University Press, 1955 - 65.

Wiese, Benno von. Lessing, Dichtung, Aesthetik, Philosophie, Leipzig, 1931.

Wimsatt, William K. and Brooks, Cleanth. Literary Criticism; a Short History, New York, 1957.

Winckelmann, Johann Jacob. J. J. Winckelmann, Gedanken über die Nachahmung der griechischen Werke in der Malerei und Bildhauerkunst (1755), ed. Leon Mis. In Collection bilingue des classiques étrangers, Paris, n.d.

anon. "A Voyage to the Mountains of the Moon under the Equator: or Parnassus Reformed," Miscellanea Aurea: or the Golden Medley, London, 1720.